LUSCIOUS

By Kate Laud

191 Bank Street, Burlington VT 05401
ISBN 978-0-9657144-8-8

Contents

Breakfast
Blueberry Muffins 9
Pecan Coffee Cake 11
Cranberry Pecan Muffins 12
Strata 13
Strawberry Marmalade 14

Soups
Dad's Tortilla Soup 17
Leslie Mandel's Jewish Chicken Soup 19
Split Pea and Ham Soup 21
Mexican Chicken Soup 22

Salads
Cole Slaw 25
Cucumber Salad 27
Fusilli Salad with Summer Sausage 29
Salade Nicoise 31
Basic Dijon Vinaigrette 32
Mrs. Massengill's Salad Dressing 33

Entrees
Classic Mac & Cheese with Vermont Cheddar 37
Flank Steak Satay 39
Onion Panade 41
Paella 43
Pasta Putanesca 45
Spicy Fried Chicken 47
Brisket 48
Black Bean Burgers 49
Chicken Chili 50
Chicken and Rice 51
Mojo Pork 52
Pan Quiche 53
Portable Chicken 54
Vegetable Lasagne 55

Sweets
Almond Thumbprint Cookies 59
Apple Pie 61
Chocolate Sugar-Dusted Cookies 63
Chocolate Raspberry Cheesecake Brownies ... 65
Chocolate Stout Cake 67
Dewars Apple Cake 69
Fig Cookies 71
Lemon Layer Cake 73
Peanut Butter & Jelly Swirl Blondies 75
Popcorn Balls from Cranny 77
Terry Delano's Hot Fudge Sauce 79
Applejack Bars 80
Butterscotch Candy 81
Carrot Cake 82
St George's Day Cookie Bars 83

Bread
Baguettes 87
Banana Bread 89
SS France Croissants 91

Sides
Baked Apples 95
Jalapeno Red Onion Relish 97
Mahogany Baked Beans 99
Fried Rice 100
Rosemary Roast Potatoes 101
Sauteed Broccoli 102

Holiday
Hazelnut Raspberry Bouche de Noel 105
    Bouche de Noel Filling and Frosting 106
    Bouche de Noel Meringue Mushrooms ... 107
Cranberry Relish Vermont Style 109
Mushroom and Green Bean Casserole 111
Roast Beef with Crispy Potatoes 113
Cranberry Cornbread Stuffing 114
Lobster Bisque 115
Stuffed Mushrooms 116

Introduction

This book is a curation of the recipes I saved from over 24 years of cooking for my family. If you do the math, that's over 7,000 dinners, and lord knows how many dirty dishes, but I suppose that's why we have children.

The way I determined which recipes to include was simple. Anytime I heard, "Mom, this is great," I saved that recipe. I've lost a few, but before I lose the rest, I'm taking them out of the looseleaf binder and packing them into this book.

Some recipes were given to me by friends. Some are taken verbatim from favorite cookbook authors. Some, I butchered, streamlined or just kinda made up. Some are sweet. Some are savory.

All were served with love.

> Special thanks is due to friends including Leslie Mandel, Terry Delano and Susan Massengill for sharing their recipes with me, to Oliver Parini for all the photographs and to Lisa Cadieux of Liquid Studio for her design expertise.

BREAKFAST

Blueberry Muffins

MAKES 12 MUFFINS

INGREDIENTS

3 cups flour

1 Tablespoon baking powder

½ teaspoon baking soda

½ teaspoon salt

10 Tablespoons butter, softened

1 cup sugar

2 large eggs

1½ cup sour cream or yogurt

2 cups blueberries

1 Tablespoon confectioner's sugar

zest of 1 lemon

¼ cup sugar for topping

vegetable oil spray

EQUIPMENT

measuring spoons (1 teaspoon, ½ teaspoon, 1 Tablespoon)

measuring cups (1 cup, ½ cup, ¼ cup)

whisk

mixer and bowl

medium bowl for flour

small bowl for lemon sugar topping

muffin tin (12 cup)

lemon zester

#12 scoop

Preheat the oven to 425°F. Coat a standard 12-cup muffin tin with vegetable oil spray.

Stir lemon zest and topping sugar together in small bowl. Set aside.

Whisk flour, baking powder, baking soda and salt together in a medium bowl. Set aside.

Using a mixer, beat the butter and sugar together until light and fluffy. Add the eggs, one at a time, beating well after each addition.

Reduce the mixer speed and beat one third of the sour cream in, then half the flour, followed by another third of the sour cream, the last of the flour and the rest of the sour cream. In a separate bowl, toss the blueberries with the confectioner's sugar. Gently fold the blueberries into the finished batter.

Portion the batter into the prepared muffin tin.

Sprinkle with lemon zest and topping sugar.

Bake 25-30 minutes until golden brown.

Don't throw away those mushy blueberries! Use them here! This recipe makes nice, puffy muffins that are crispy on top with a smack of lemon. You can freeze the batter in muffin-sized globs and bake them any morning when you have 30 minutes. Or when you get an AirBNB guest.

Pecan Coffee Cake

SERVES 8

INGREDIENTS

2 cups flour

¼ teaspoon salt

1 Tablespoon baking powder

¼ cup pecans, processed into crumbs

1 cup butter, softened

1½ cups sugar

1 cup sour cream

2 large eggs

1 Tablespoon vanilla

2 Tablespoons butter

1 cup chopped pecans, lightly toasted

½ cup brown sugar

1 teaspoon cinnamon

vegetable oil spray

EQUIPMENT

measuring spoons
(1 teaspoon, ¼ teaspoon, 1 Tablespoon)

measuring cups
(1 cup, ½ cup, ¼ cup)

whisk

1 quart-sized bowl for dry ingredients

mixer and larger bowl

chef's knife and cutting board

parchment

9"x 13" baking pan

toothpick

Preheat the oven to 350°F.

Coat a 9"x 13" pan with vegetable oil spray and line it with a 9"x 17" sheet of wax paper or parchment paper so the paper hangs over the 9" ends of the pan.

Whisk together the flour, salt, baking powder and ground pecans in a small bowl and set aside.

Mix the butter and sugar until smooth. Add sour cream and beat until combined. Beat in one egg at a time. Add vanilla.

Add the flour mixture to the butter mixture.

Don't worry if the batter is lumpy. Pour batter into prepared pan. (The engineers use a level here. No, they don't.)

Combine the butter, pecans, brown sugar and cinnamon and microwave for 10 seconds. Stir.

Spread this evenly over the batter.

Bake for 35 minutes or until a toothpick comes out with only a crumb or two.

Charlie loved this coffee cake. This recipe substitutes finely ground pecans for some of the flour, giving the cake a nutty richness and a "fall apart" texture. It is adapted from a website called Cooking for Engineers *(marvelously technical) but simplified here.*

Cranberry Pecan Muffins

MAKES 12 MUFFINS

INGREDIENTS

3 Tablespoons flour

4 teaspoons granulated sugar

1 Tablespoon packed light brown sugar

2 Tablespoons unsalted butter, cut into ½" pieces, softened

pinch salt

½ cup pecan halves

1⅓ cups flour

1½ teaspoons baking powder

¾ teaspoon salt

1¼ cups pecan halves, toasted and cooled

1 cup plus 1 Tablespoon sugar

2 eggs

6 Tablespoons unsalted butter, melted and cooled slightly

½ cup whole milk

2 cups fresh cranberries

1 Tablespoon confectioner's sugar

vegetable oil spray

EQUIPMENT

measuring spoons (1 Tablespoon, 1 teaspoon, ½ teaspoon, ¼ teaspoon)

measuring cups (1 cup, ⅓ cup, ¼ cup)

mixing bowl

whisk

food processor

ice cream scoop or large soup spoon

muffin tin

Preheat oven to 425°F.

Process flour, granulated sugar, brown sugar, butter, and salt in food processor until mixture resembles coarse sand. Add ½ cup pecans and process until pecans are coarsely chopped. Transfer to small bowl and use as streusel topping.

Coat 12-cup muffin tin with vegetable oil spray.

Whisk together rest of flour, baking powder, ½ teaspoon salt. Set aside.

Process toasted pecans and granulated sugar until mixture resembles sand. Transfer to large bowl and whisk in eggs, butter, and milk until combined. Whisk flour mixture into egg mixture until just moistened. Let batter rest 30 minutes.

Pulse cranberries, remaining ¼ teaspoon salt, and confectioner's sugar in food processor until coarsely chopped. Fold into batter and scoop batter into muffin tin.

Sprinkle on streusel topping, gently pressing to adhere.

Bake until muffin tops are golden, about 18 minutes.

Cool ten minutes in tin and ten minutes after released from tin.

We took these to Nana's for Thanksgiving 2011.

Strata

SERVES 8-10

INGREDIENTS

1 dozen eggs

2 cups milk, half and half or cream

8-12 ounces grated cheese

torn or sliced bread, about 8-10 slices

1 pound cooked sausage, ham or bacon

onions, tomatoes, potatoes, peppers, parsley, basil (optional)

½ teaspoons salt

1 teaspoon pepper

1 teaspoon ground dry mustard

vegetable oil spray

EQUIPMENT

whisk

medium glass bowl

measuring spoons (1 teaspoon, ½ teaspoon)

measuring cups (1 cup)

saute pan to cook sausage or bacon

rectangular oven-proof dish, as for lasagne

Coat a rectangular pan with vegetable oil spray.

Whisk eggs thoroughly in medium bowl and add salt, pepper and mustard. Whisk again.

Add milk and cheese and stir to combine.

Layer bread slices or pieces in baking dish. Layer sausage, ham or bacon on top of bread.

Pour egg mixture thoroughly on top of bread and meat.

Cover with plastic wrap and refrigerate overnight.

In the morning, preheat oven to 350°F.

Unwrap baking dish and bake for 50 minutes or until golden brown.

Breakfast is my favorite meal because there's so little planning required. To keep it simple, you can throw together a strata the night before. Use leftover onions (saute them first), however many eggs you have, whatever cheese is on hand, chunks of breakfast meats or even tomatoes and potatoes. I'll never forget a Garden Club planning meeting where one member suggested that the menu for the next lunch meeting be STRATA. Just strata. She was greeted with a few disturbed glances Not only was it a great lunch, no two were the same.

Strawberry Marmalade

YIELD 8 PINTS

INGREDIENTS

4 pounds strawberries, cleaned, trimmed and cut into halves

2 lemons, peel cut into thin strips

juice of 2 lemons

1 box or package of fruit pectin

7 cups sugar

8 half pint jars

EQUIPMENT

large pot, like for corn on the cob, big enough to boil 8 glass jars at one time

large pot for boiling fruit (at least 2 quarts)

8 glass jars and lids

ladle for filling jars

tongs for removing jars from boiling water

paper towels for cleaning hot jam off jars and for laying under filled jars

potholders

labels (the best part)

Boil jars and lids in large pot to sterilize. Don't do this too long in advance because the jars should be warm when you are filling them with jam or they will crack.

If using lemon peel, boil the peel in the medium-sized pot just covered with water for 5 minutes then drain out the water, keeping the peel in the pot.

Add berries and lemon juice to the pot. Add pectin. Mix well. Bring to a rolling boil. Stir constantly. Add all the sugar. Boil hard, stirring occasionally, for 20 minutes.

Test doneness by ladling a small amount of jam onto a plate and drawing a spoon through the jam. If the "path" stays clear, the jam can be jarred at this point.

Remove the jam from heat. Skim foam off as it cools. Ladle jam into jars.

Wet a bit of a clean paper towel to wipe jam from jar rims, being careful not to endanger the sterility of the jars.

Tighten lids "finger tight," not terribly overtight.

Put jars back into large pot full of boiling water and boil them for 10 minutes.

Remove jars from water and place on dish towel to dry.

One summer, after our Pick Your Own orgy at Mazza's, we made enough jam to last till Christmas.

SOUP

Dad's Tortilla Soup

SERVES 6

INGREDIENTS

2 Tablespoons olive oil

1 half yellow onion, (not Vidalia) chopped

¼ cup celery, chopped

1 jalapeno, chopped

1 carton chicken broth (32 ounces total)

½ cup tomato sauce

1 can of chicken (looks like a can of tuna)

½ cup (2 ounces) shredded monterey jack cheese (or mild cheddar)

1 cup chopped fresh cilantro

crushed tortilla chips or sliced, toasted tortillas

1 ripe avocado

jalapeno slices (optional)

salt

EQUIPMENT

soup pot (4 quart saucepan)

measuring spoons (1 Tablespoon)

measuring cups (1 cup, ¼ cup)

chef's knife and cutting board

ladle

six soup bowls

Heat the oil over medium heat and add onions, celery and jalapeno.

Saute until onions are translucent.

Add chicken broth, tomato sauce and chicken and bring to a boil.

Remove soup from heat and stir in cheese.

Before ladling soup into bowls, place 2-3 tortilla chips in the bottom of each bowl.

Garnish with cilantro, avocado and jalapeno slices.

Think back to a cold January night at our house on Fox Hollow Road. Everyone is tired. Homework is done. The kitchen smells like onions are cooking. You know Dad is in charge of dinner, and you are hoping he's making Dinner #3.

Leslie Mandel's Jewish Chicken Soup

SERVES 6

INGREDIENTS

1 chicken

carrots

onion or leeks

celery

Manischewitz egg noodles

salt and pepper, to taste

EQUIPMENT

big pot that can go from oven to stovetop

rubber gloves

tongs

chef's knife and cutting board

Take a chicken (it's okay if it's frozen.) Put it in a pot. Cover it with water. Boil uncovered about 30 minutes if it's fresh, or until the meat is no longer pink. Boil an hour or so if it is frozen. Skim the bubbly stuff that rises to the top and discard it. Remove from heat and let cool long enough to handle the meat after you remove the chicken from the pot. I like to use rubber gloves for this. (Rubber chicken gloves :›)

Tear the chicken meat off the bones. Get the easy stuff, like the breast and thigh meat. Don't struggle with the gristly stuff. You'll have enough meat without it. Put the meat in a container in the fridge. Make sure there's no cartilage or bones in the meat. It should be just the good parts, like for a chicken salad. Take the bones and put them back in the pot. Add enough fresh water to cover the carcass and bring it to a boil, uncovered. As soon as it boils, turn it down to a simmer. Simmer for at least an hour. The longer you simmer, the deeper the flavor. Some people simmer this all day.

Remove the pot from the heat. Remove the carcass and stray bits of chicken and throw them away.

Strain the remaining broth into a heat-proof and fridge-proof container, like a stainless steel bowl or pot. You can use a paper towel folded into a double-triangle like a coffee filter, cheese cloth or a gauzy kitchen towel for straining.

Cool the strained broth until the fat has risen to the top of the container and remove it with a spoon. (You can save time if you put it in the freezer.) Put the container on low heat. Add onion, carrot and celery. Add egg noodles. Simmer about 30 minutes. The vegetables should sweeten and flavor the broth without getting mushy. Add salt and pepper to taste. Just before serving, add back the chicken meat.

Mom's short cut: buy a hot, roasted chicken or bake a chicken for 1½ hours. Tear off the meat and add it to 4 cups of hot chicken broth with any of the above vegetables and simmer 10 minutes.

Nobody does it better.

Split Pea and Ham Soup

SERVES 4-6

INGREDIENTS

2 Tablespoons unsalted butter

2 garlic cloves, minced

1 large onion, chopped fine

½ teaspoon salt

8 cups water

2 chicken bouillon cubes

1 pound ham, diced

3 slices bacon

1 pound dry green peas

2 carrots

1 celery stalk

salt and pepper, to taste

EQUIPMENT

measuring spoons (1 Tablespoon, ½ teaspoon)

measuring cups (1 cup)

chef's knife and cutting board

Dutch oven

Heat butter in Dutch oven until melted.

Add onion and ½ teaspoon salt and cook until onions are translucent.

Add garlic and cook for a minute.

Add water, bouillon cubes, ham, bacon and peas.

Increase heat to high and once boiling, cover and simmer, stirring attentively to keep peas from sticking to the bottom for about 45 minutes.

Stir in carrots and celery and cook additional 30 minutes.

This soup makes a great dinner along with a fresh hunk of bread and an apple for dessert.

Mexican Chicken Soup

SERVES 4-6

INGREDIENTS

1 jar green salsa, such as Mrs. Renfro's, mild to medium

4 cups water

4 chicken bouillon cubes

juice of one lime

1 garlic clove, minced

4 chicken thighs, preferably with bones

1-2 handfuls of chopped kale or spinach

Optional Ingredients

2-3 sweet potatoes, microwaved for 7 minutes, peeled and cubed

1-2 ears of corn, kernels only

1 avocado, sliced

½ cup cilantro, chopped

2 Tablespoons sour cream

EQUIPMENT

large saucepan

immersion or traditional blender

chef's knife and cutting board

measuring spoons (1 Tablespoon)

measuring cups (1 cup, ½ cup)

Put everything except the garnishes in a saucepan and turn heat to medium high.

When the soup reaches a boil, turn it down to low and simmer for one hour, covered. After an hour, remove the chicken pieces.

Pull the chicken meat from the bones and set meat aside in the fridge. Let the soup cool off the stove.

Once cool, buzz the soup for 15 seconds with an immersion blender or put 2 cups of the soup into a traditional blender, puree and add back to the pot.

Add the chicken meat back to the pot and reheat the soup over low heat until ready to serve.

Garnish with cilantro sprigs, avocado and sour cream.

Quote from the kitchen the first time this soup was served, "If this was all I had to eat for the rest of my life, I'd be happy." Gratitude goes to Julia Buteux for sending me Against All Grain, *an amazing cookbook by Danielle Walker. This recipe is adapted from her gorgeous work.*

As with most soups, many ingredients are optional. The salsa and chicken are the key elements. Everything else just deepens the flavor. I've made this recipe with both mild and medium salsa and medium is much better.

SALADS

Cole Slaw

SERVES 6

INGREDIENTS

2 heads cabbage, one green and one red

2 radishes, sliced thinly into disks (optional)

1½ cup rice or white wine vinegar

1 cup sugar

1 teaspoon salt

1 teaspoon pepper

1 scoop mayonnaise (optional)

2 Tablespoons light olive oil

EQUIPMENT

chef's knife and cutting board

measuring spoons (1 Tablespoon, 1 teaspoon)

measuring cups (1 cup, ½ cup)

large serving bowl

serving spoon

Slice off the stem end of the cabbage and then slice the head in half from top to bottom. Slice each half again from top to bottom. Trim the stem end by cutting it out diagonally from each of the 4 quarters. Throw away any loose outer leaves.

Slice each quarter by placing a flat side on the cutting board and slicing north-south as thinly as you can. Once you have a pile of parallel slices, slice them east-west. Lastly, slice them along the north-south lines again, shredding them as you go.

Slice the radishes.

Put the cabbage and radish into a large bowl and mix thoroughly.

To make the dressing, mix the sugar with the vinegar. Season lightly with salt and pepper and add the oil. You can heat the dressing if the sugar does not completely dissolve.

Add a scoop of mayonnaise if you want a creamier slaw.

Let the cabbage marinate in the dressing for at least a half hour. If making cole slaw for the next day, keep the cabbage "undressed" until right before serving or the green and red mixture will combine to be uniformly pink.

The familiar, never-fail omnipresent side dish.

It's amazing how easy it is to make this taste great with just vinegar and sugar. In fact, if you have "seasoned" rice vinegar (with added sugar) that and a little salt is all you need.

Cucumber Salad

SERVES 6

INGREDIENTS

4 cucumbers, sliced and partly peeled, drained well

1 teaspoon white or black pepper, but white preferred

½ teaspoon salt

1 clove garlic, minced

1 cup plain Greek yogurt, either low fat or full fat

½ cup mayonnaise (optional)

1 radish, sliced (optional)

2 Tablespoons cilantro, chopped (optional)

EQUIPMENT

mixing bowl

measuring spoons (1 teaspoon, ½ teaspoon)

measuring cups (1 cup, ½ cup)

chef's knife and cutting board

small salad bowl

Slice the cucumbers and sprinkle them lightly with salt. Allow them to drain while you make the dressing.

Mix garlic, yogurt and mayonnaise with salt and pepper.

Combine cucumbers with dressing at the last minute.

Garnish and serve.

Dad introduced this to our family as "tzatziki." He would prefer more garlic and would substitute sour cream for the mayonnaise, but I'm varying the recipe to make some room for your WASP heritage. This is better the second day, so either make the dressing a day ahead or really drain the water out of the cucumbers. I like using white pepper if you have it because it keeps the sauce really white.

Fusilli Salad with Summer Sausage

SERVES 4-6

INGREDIENTS

6 Tablespoons extra virgin olive oil

1 cup sun-dried tomatoes, chopped (oil-soaked or dry)

¼ cup white wine vinegar

1 garlic clove, minced

1 Tablespoon plus ½ teaspoon salt

½ teaspoon pepper

1 pound fusilli or any curly-shaped pasta

1½ ounces spinach

8 ounces summer sausage, cut into bite-sized chunks

1 cup provolone, cut into bite-sized chunks

½ cup Kalamata olives, chopped

EQUIPMENT

measuring spoons (1 Tablespoon, ½ teaspoon)

measuring cups (1 cup, ½ cup, ¼ cup)

chef's knife and cutting board

whisk

pasta pot, at least 4 quart size

strainer

large salad bowl

Bring 4 quarts water to boil in large pot.

Whisk olive oil, sun-dried tomatoes, vinegar, garlic, ½ teaspoon salt and the pepper together in bowl large enough to hold entire pasta salad.

Add fusilli and 1 tablespoon salt to boiling water and cook, stirring often, until soft.

Drain, shaking off excess water. (This is a lot of salt, but it really helps flavor the salad.)

Add hot, drained fusilli and spinach to bowl with dressing and toss.

Cover and refrigerate until cooled, about 15 minutes.

Just before serving, stir in sausage, provolone, and olives, and season with salt and pepper to taste.

Charlie was a fan of this salad! It balances the bite of a strong vinaigrette with the salty brine of olives and sun-dried tomatoes nuanced by the nuttiness of slightly melted provolone and the garlicky spice of summer sausage.

Salade Niçoise

SERVES 8

INGREDIENTS

1 pound red-skinned potatoes, quartered

4 large eggs, hard boiled and sliced or quartered

10 ounces thin green beans, trimmed

¼ cup white wine vinegar

½ shallot, minced (about 2 Tablespoons)

2 Tablespoons Dijon mustard

pepper, to taste

¾ cup extra virgin olive oil

salt, to taste

1 head Boston lettuce, leaves separated

8 cherry tomatoes or small cocktail tomatoes, halved or quartered

6 radishes, trimmed and quartered

½ cup nicoise olives

2 Tablespoons capers

2 5½ ounce cans really good tuna (or a cooked tuna steak)

EQUIPMENT

measuring spoons (1 Tablespoon)

measuring cups (½ cup, ¼ cup)

chef's knife and cutting board

8 salad plates

Boil potatoes and set aside.

Boil eggs and set aside.

Trim and steam green beans and set aside.

Mix vinegar, shallot, mustard, pepper and olive oil and set aside.

Tear lettuce and mix with tomatoes, radishes and olives.

Slice tuna.

Compose salad on 8 plates separating lettuce mixture, tuna, green beans and potatoes. Add egg pieces in center of plate.

Pour dressing lightly over everything.

The dressing in this salad is incredible. I'm sure it could be used on other things, but it is clearly identifiable as a nicoise dressing. Some recipes insist on dressing everything separately, but you can dress it all at once. You can also plop it all together in a big bowl and serve it like a classic salad, but it is traditionally served plated.

Basic Dijon Vinaigrette

SERVES 4-6

INGREDIENTS

3 Tablespoon oil

1 Tablespoon lemon juice or red wine vinegar

1 teaspoon Dijon mustard

1 Tablespoon minced shallots or red onion

1 teaspoon sugar

1 teaspoon salt or to taste

EQUIPMENT

measuring spoons (1 Tablespoon, 1 teaspoon)

whisk or fork

salad dressing jar

Instructions vary as to whether to use a ratio of 3:1 or 4:1 oil to acid in a dressing. If you are willing to take the time to really emulsify (mix, stir or whisk) the acid ingredients, you should only need 3 measures of oil to every measure of acid. If you are lazier, use 4 because you'll need that much more oil to counteract the pools of unblended acid flavors.

Emulsifiers include mayonnaise, mustard and raw egg yolk. Egg yolk is the best because it has the right fats to hold the oil and acid together the longest. Not many people trust raw egg yolk these days. Mayonnaise works too, but only because egg yolk is one ingredient. (It's pasteurized, so the yolk is not raw.) Dijon mustard is my favorite.

You can add other seasonings, like paprika, salt, pepper, oregano, basil or minced sun-dried tomatoes, but the ratio of fat to acid still holds.

Instead of oil, you may wish to use peanut butter, tahini, mayonnaise, parmesan cheese, buttermilk or cream. Acids can be citrus juice, soy sauce or any vinegar. Seasonings can be raw or roasted garlic, pepper, ginger or sugar for cole slaw.

Mrs. Massengill's Salad Dressing

SERVES 6

INGREDIENTS

½ teaspoon sugar

½ teaspoon pepper

1 teaspoon salt

1 clove garlic, minced or grated (optional in my opinion)

2 Tablespoons white wine vinegar

1½ Tablespoons lemon juice

6 Tablespoons olive oil

EQUIPMENT

measuring spoons (½ teaspoon, 1 teaspoon, 1 Tablespoon)

garlic press

whisk

salad dressing jar

Seven ingredients.

Five minutes.

Memorize this!

Whisk all ingredients together and serve.

Bow down to Susan Massengill for giving us her mother, Joanne Davis' salad dressing recipe. She gave me this recipe reluctantly, so please credit her every time you use it! The recipe has been taped inside our pantry door since 1997.

ENTREES

Classic Mac & Cheese with Vermont Cheddar

SERVES 6-8

INGREDIENTS

leftover white bread, toasted and chopped into rough pieces

5 Tablespoons butter

1 pound elbow macaroni

1 Tablespoon salt

3 Tablespoons butter (cold), cut into pieces

2 Tablespoons cornstarch

⅓ cup Vermont cheese powder*

1½ teaspoon Dijon mustard

½ teaspoon cayenne (optional)

1 cup milk

16 ounces sharp Vermont cheddar cheese, crumbled (4 cups)

EQUIPMENT

measuring spoons (1 Tablespoon, 1 teaspoon, ½ teaspoon)

measuring cups (1 cup, ⅓ cup)

Dutch oven

colander

chef's knife and cutting board

large skillet

whisk

13"x 9" baking dish

Preheat oven to 350°F.

Bring 4 quarts water to boil in Dutch oven over high heat. Add macaroni and 1 Tablespoon salt; cook until pasta is tender.

Drain pasta in colander and set aside.

Return Dutch oven to stove and heat 3 Tablespoons butter over medium-heat until foaming.

In a separate bowl, stir cornstarch into cold milk until it dissolves.

Pour milk mixture into butter and stir in cheese powder, mustard and cayenne. Turn heat to low and add cheese.

Stir, add pasta and stir again.

Pour mixture into 13"x 9" baking pan or two small 8" square pans.

Chop toast crumbs with the remaining 2 Tablespoons cold butter and sprinkle evenly over the macaroni.

Bake at 350°F for 20 minutes.

When ready to serve, broil until crumbs are deep golden brown, 3-5 minutes, rotating pan if necessary for even browning.

Cool about 5 minutes, then serve.

*Vermont cheese powder is made by King Arthur Flour (...or substitute grated parmesan.)

You can argue that this recipe is too rich, but it taste way better than boxed mac and cheese. Save the ends of good bread and the last bits of good cheese in the freezer so you can use them up in this recipe. Nana makes this without the milk step, just stirring grated cheddar into hot noodles. This recipe takes longer, but is more classic. Don't skimp on the seasoning, since the pasta tends to soak up the bite of the cheese. Like many recipes incorporating seasonings with dairy products, the taste improves over time.

Flank Steak Satay

SERVES 6

INGREDIENTS

Marinade

2 Tablespoons oil

2 Tablespoons brown sugar

1 Tablespoon fish sauce

1-2 pounds flank steak, cut into ¼" thick slices

Glaze

1 Tablespoon oil

2 Tablespoons Thai red curry paste

1 Tablespoon brown sugar

2 garlic cloves, minced

1 150ml can coconut milk

⅓ cup peanut butter

juice of 2 limes

1 Tablespoon fish sauce

½ teaspoon salt

¼ cup peanuts, chopped

EQUIPMENT

measuring spoons (1 teaspoon, 1 Tablespoon)

measuring cups (1 cup, ⅓ cup)

10-12 skewers

grill

mixing bowl

whisk

Pint-sized mason jar

garlic press

Whisk oil, sugar, and fish sauce together in zip lock bag. Toss beef with marinade and let stand at room temperature for 30 minutes.

Weave beef onto skewers, leaving a few inches at bottom of skewer exposed.

Place beef skewers on very hot grill and cook about 3 minutes. Flip skewers and cook until the meat takes on a burnished look, about 3 more minutes.

For the glaze, combine all ingredients except peanuts and microwave for 60-90 seconds.

Stir in peanuts and pour the glaze over the full dish of skewers or serve it on the side.

I made this for a few Keewaydin staffmen who came for a July lakeside dinner and for Maisie when she brought her roommate Emily home from Boston. There are more ingredients than you'd need for a burgers and dogs barbeque, but since you eat these with your hands, it feels right for a lazy summer picnic. The beef takes on a delicious burnished glaze once it starts to cook. As Rhiannon taught me, go easy on the fish sauce.

Onion Panade

SERVES 4-6

INGREDIENTS

2 Tablespoons olive oil

1½ pounds onions (about four cups, sliced), peeled and sliced

2-3 thyme sprigs (or kale, spinach, chard or herb)

⅓ loaf day old country style bread, sliced

⅓ cup Parmesan cheese

⅓ cup Gruyere cheese

3-4 cups chicken or vegetable, or beef broth

2 Tablespoons butter

EQUIPMENT

baking sheet

saute pan

2 quart baking dish

measuring spoons (1 Tablespoon)

measuring cups (1 cup, ⅓ cup)

Preheat oven to 350°F.

Heat oil in saute pan and add onions. Cook over medium low heat until quite soft, about 30 minutes. Turn the heat up slightly and cook the onions, stirring occasionally until a medium golden brown, about 15 minutes.

Add the thyme (or greens) and add salt to taste.

While onions are cooking, place the slices of bread on a baking sheet in a 350°F oven until dry but not brown, about 5 minutes.

Grate and mix two cheese together.

Make a layer of bread slices in the bottom of the baking dish. Spread of half the onions onto the bread slices and sprinkle with about ⅓ of the cheese. Make another layer of bread slices and cover with the rest of the onions and ⅓ of the cheese. Make a final layer of bread slices and sprinkle with the remaining cheese.

Heat the broth and carefully pour it into the baking dish without disturbing the layers, until the top layer of bread starts to float. Dot the top with 2 Tablespoons of butter.

Cover and bake in a 350°F oven for 45 minutes, then uncover the dish and bake for another 20-30 minutes, or until the top is golden brown and crisp.

I remember Baba begging Nana to make this dish. I always thought it was from Julia Child's Mastering the Art of French Cooking, *but it turns out it's a standard French peasant recipe kind of like French Onion Soup without the soup.*

Paella

SERVES 4-6

INGREDIENTS

4 chicken thighs, bone-in, trimmed

6 Tablespoons olive oil

½ teaspoon salt

½ teaspoon pepper

1 pound chorizo

5-10 jumbo shrimp

3 Tablespoons tomato paste

4 cloves garlic, sliced

2 teaspoons paprika

4 cups chicken broth

8 ounces clam juice

Pinch saffron

1 cup chopped shallots

3 cups Arborio rice

1 cup jarred red peppers

1 cup frozen peas

EQUIPMENT

paella pan or deep roasting pan

tongs

2 quart saute pan

chef's knife and cutting board

measuring spoons (1 teaspoon, ½ teaspoon, 1 Tablespoon)

measuring cups (1 cup)

Coat chicken with 1 Tablespoon oil, salt and pepper. Grill chicken and remove skin.

Grill chorizo and slice.

Coat shrimp with 1 Tablespoon oil and refrigerate.

In saucepan, toast tomato paste with 2 Tablespoons oil, garlic and paprika. Add broth, clam juice and saffron. Bring to a boil, stir and set aside.

Warm 2 Tablespoons oil in paella pan on 400°F grill.

Add shallots and saute for 5 minutes.

Add rice and red peppers and stir to coat. Top rice with chicken, sausage and shrimp.

Gently pour broth mixture over the rice.

Close grill and cook at 400°F for 20 minutes. Lower grill temperature to 300°F and cook an additional 20 minutes or until liquid is boiled off.

Sprinkle peas over rice and cook 5 minutes more.

Remove from grill and serve.

This is a nice change from more familiar grilled meals. It takes a few trips to the grill and requires some kitchen prep, but the leftovers are worth it.

Pasta Putanesca

SERVES 6-8

INGREDIENTS

1 pound dried spaghetti or angel hair (capellini)

1 teaspoon salt

5 garlic cloves, forced through a garlic press

½ cup extra virgin olive oil

1 28 ounces can whole tomatoes in juice (preferably Italian)

2 teaspoons anchovy paste

pinch of sugar (optional)

½ teaspoon red pepper flakes

½ cup pitted Kalamata olives

2 Tablespoons drained capers

½ cup coarsely chopped basil

EQUIPMENT

spaghetti pot and strainer

saucepan

garlic press or chef's knife

measuring spoons (1 Tablespoon, 1 teaspoon, ½ teaspoon)

measuring cups (1 cup, ½ cup)

Boil the pasta with the salt.

Saute garlic in ¼ cup of oil over medium low heat for one minute.

Add tomatoes and anchovy paste and simmer until sauce turns from bright red to burnished red, about 5-10 minutes.

Add sugar and stir well.

Drain pasta and toss in serving bowl with ¼ cup olive oil.

Add sauce.

Add red pepper flakes, olives and capers and toss well.

Garnish with basil.

Serve hot.

This recipe has no fresh ingredients, so it's perfect for a night when your fridge is bare. The literal translation is close to "garbage pasta" or, more fun, "prostitute pasta," perhaps because it's hot, delicious, easy and fast. Dad likes it because it's cheap. He adds chopped, marinated artichokes and throws in a few pignoli nuts, but here's the original 1950s recipe.

Spicy Fried Chicken

SERVES 4-6

INGREDIENTS

½ cup Frank's hot sauce

½ cup salt

½ cup sugar

4 chicken breasts, bone-in, skin removed

2 quarts water

1 teaspoon cayenne pepper

½ teaspoon paprika

1½ teaspoon salt

½ teaspoon pepper

½ teaspoon garlic powder

2 teaspoons sugar, honey or maple syrup

¼ cup vegetable oil for spicy sauce

2 cups flour

½ teaspoon salt

½ teaspoon pepper

2 quarts vegetable oil

EQUIPMENT

large container for marinating chicken

pie plate for dredging

wire rack and rimmed roasting pan

Dutch oven

tongs

measuring cups (1 cup, ¼ cup)

measuring spoons (1 teaspoon, ½ teaspoon)

Whisk hot sauce, salt, and sugar in large bowl.

Add chicken. Add water until chicken is fully submerged.

Refrigerate, covered, for 30 minutes to an 1 hour.

Mix cayenne, paprika, 1½ teaspoon salt, pepper, garlic powder, sugar and oil. Microwave for 40 seconds.

Combine flour, ½ teaspoon salt, and pepper in large bowl.

Remove chicken from marinade and dredge in flour mixture. Transfer to wire rack. Set aside excess seasoned flour.

Warm oven to 200°F.

Heat remaining oil in large Dutch oven.

Recoat chicken in reserved seasoned flour. Fry half of chicken in Dutch oven over medium heat until golden brown, 20-25 minutes.

Drain chicken on clean wire rack over roasting pan and place in warm oven until ready to serve.

Stir spicy oil mixture to recombine and brush over both sides of chicken before serving.

Because sometimes you need serious comfort food.

Brisket

SERVES 6

INGREDIENTS

1/3 cup brown sugar

3 Tablespoons paprika

3 Tablespoons salt

3 Tablespoons pepper

2 Tablespoons cumin

3 pounds of beef brisket

EQUIPMENT

Dutch oven or roasting pan with cover

measuring spoons (1 Tablespoon)

measuring cups (⅓ cup)

1 quart bowl for spices

foil

chef's knife and cutting board

skillet (optional)

parchment paper

Combine the spices and pour half of the mixture on a sheet of parchment. Lay the brisket on the spices and pat the rest of the spice mixture on top.

Wrap the meat in foil and refrigerate overnight.

In the morning, sear the meat before roasting it in the oven. You can do this on the grill or on the stove. If you're using the stove, unwrap the meat, heat a skillet to high and brown the meat for 5 minutes per side. If you're using the grill, unwrap the meat, heat the grill to 400°F and cook each side of the meat, fat side up first, for 20 minutes.

After searing, put the meat in a covered pot and cook for 10-12 hours at 225°F.

Searing is optional. If you want to skip that step, just put the brisket in a 225°F oven first thing in the morning. Keep it in the original foil wrapping in a covered pot in the oven. Leave it alone to cook for 10 to 12 hours.

Unwrap, slice and serve.

We've had brisket many different ways, but you ate this one for breakfast, lunch and dinner. Brisket tastes like it takes talent, but any meat you cook for 12 hours will have that "cut it with a fork" texture. Amp up the sweet, smoky taste by using a dry spice rub and skip the messy sauces. This rub is based on "Cheaters Brisket" from The New York Times. *It cooks in foil so cleanup is minimal.*

Black Bean Burgers

MAKES 6-8 PATTIES

INGREDIENTS

1 can black beans, drained but still goopy

1 cup stuffing mix, processed into crumbs

2 eggs, whisked

2 Tablespoons Frank's hot sauce

1 Tablespoon cumin

¼ cup grated onion

4 Tablespoons uncooked chia seeds

2 Tablespoons anchovy paste, optional

1 fresh jalapeno, diced

2 Tablespoons oil

EQUIPMENT

measuring spoons (1 Tablespoon)

measuring cups (1 cup, ¼ cup)

ice cream scoop

medium sized bowl

fork

baking sheet

parchment

skillet

potato masher

#2 scoop

parchment paper

Mash the beans until they almost have the texture of refried beans. Stir in remaining ingredients, mashing up any larger stuffing or jalapeno pieces.

Using an ice cream scoop, place uniform sized balls on a parchment-lined baking sheet. Press each one into a 3" diameter patty with straight sides.

At this point, the patties can be frozen or refrigerated for several days.

To cook, add oil to skillet over medium heat. Cook patties for 2-3 minutes until brown then flip and cook an additional 2 minutes until warm throughout.

Remember the homemade hamburger buns that I served with these burgers? Forgive me for using some pre-packaged ingredients, but this is how I made the burgers you loved.

Chicken Chili

SERVES 6-8

INGREDIENTS

4 chicken breast halves, boneless and skinless

salt and pepper

5 Tablespoons oil

1 Jalapeno chili, minced (remove seeds first)

2 medium onions, chopped

2 garlic cloves, minced

1 Tablespoon ground cumin

¼ teaspoon salt

2 14½ ounce cans cannellini beans, drained and rinsed

3 cups chicken broth

2 Tablespoons fresh lime juice (from 2 to 3 limes)

sliced scallions, grated cheddar, cilantro, sour cream, lime wedges, tortilla chips (all optional)

EQUIPMENT

Dutch oven

tongs

plate

chef's knife

stick blender

instant read thermometer

measuring spoons (1 Tablespoon, ¼ teaspoon)

Season chicken with salt and pepper.

Heat 3 Tablespoons oil in large Dutch oven over medium-high heat until oil begins to spread thin.

Add chicken breasts, meaty side down and brown them without moving them about 4 minutes.

Using tongs, lift the chicken, add another 2 Tablespoons oil to the pot, replace the chicken and brown the other side for about 2 minutes.

Transfer chicken to plate.

Reduce heat to medium. Add ⅔ of the minced jalapeno, the onions, garlic, cumin and ¼ teaspoon salt, stirring gently until onions soften, about 10 minutes.

Remove pot from heat and add 1 cup beans and 1 cup broth and blend with a stick blender until smooth, about 20 seconds.

Add remaining broth, and add back the chicken. Bring to boil over medium-high heat. Reduce heat to a simmer, stirring occasionally, until chicken registers 160°F.

Transfer chicken to large clean plate.

Stir in remaining beans and continue to simmer until beans are heated through and chili has thickened slightly, about 10 minutes.

When the cooked chicken has cooled slightly, shred it and add it with the lime juice, optional ingredients, and remaining minced jalapeno to the pot and simmer.

Adjust seasonings with salt and pepper and serve.

This chili is great for a Superbowl party or a meal that leaves leftovers.

Chicken and Rice

SERVES 2

INGREDIENTS

4 Tablespoons olive oil

2 chicken breasts, skinless and boneless

1 small yellow or white onion, chopped

1 garlic clove, minced (optional)

1 cup of rice, dry

2 cups water

2 chicken boullion cubes

lemon slices, zest, or 1 Tablespoon lemon juice (optional)

EQUIPMENT

measuring cups (1 cup)

chef's knife and cutting board

Dutch oven

Heat 2 Tablespoons oil in a Dutch oven on the stove at medium high heat. Brown the chicken for a minute or two, then flip it and brown the other side. Remove the chicken and set aside. Leave any chicken juices in the pot.

Add the other 2 Tablespoons oil to the pot and warm the oil over medium heat. Add the chopped onion and sauté until the onion is transparent, about 5 minutes. If using garlic, add it after the onions have been sautéed.

Pour in the rice, water and boullion cubes. If using lemon, add the lemon juice and/or zest here. Stir. Turn the heat up to high and leave the pot uncovered.

When the water begins to boil, place the chicken on top of the rice and cover the pot. Turn the heat down to low and cook about 20 minutes without removing the cover.

Garnish with lemon slices if using and serve directly from the pot.

This recipe is too easy. Even Baba learned how to make it in Morristown when he had to leave Nana behind in Key West. Substitute a can of cream of chicken soup for the water and bouillon if you want to sink that low.

Mojo Pork

SERVES 4-6

INGREDIENTS

Brine

4-5 pound bone-in pork shoulder, pierced with knife cuts

3 cups sugar

2 cups salt

2 heads fresh garlic, smashed

4 cups orange juice

water, enough to fully submerge roast

Serving Sauce

2 teaspoons salt

2 cloves garlic, minced

½ teaspoon cumin

¼ cup orange juice

¼ cup white vinegar

¼ cup olive oil

EQUIPMENT

tall pot for marinating the roast

chef's knife and cutting board

foil

grill or oven

glass bowl for microwaving serving sauce

large serving dish

measuring cups (1 cup, ¼ cup)

measuring spoons (1 teaspoon, ½ teaspoon)

Combine the sugar, salt, garlic and orange juice in a tall container and mix until the sugar is dissolved.

Submerge the pork, adding as much water as you need to keep it covered.

Cover and refrigerate. A day or two later, about 4 hours before serving, pre-heat a grill to around 400°F.

Wrap the pork loosely in foil and place it on the grill.

Turn the heat down to about 250°F and cook for 4 hours. (A boneless roast will be done in two hours.)

Check that the meat is no longer pink inside, then remove from heat and let it sit at room temperature on a serving dish while you make the serving sauce.

Mix salt, garlic and cumin into a paste and add the orange juice, vinegar and oil. Microwave for 45 seconds until warm.

Stir well and pour over pork. Serve hot.

I first made this at the lake and have tried to make it taste like taco truck carnitas. The recipe looks like an undertaking, but the "hands on" time is minimal. Start brining the pork a day or two before you want to serve it.

Pan Quiche

MAKES 24 SQUARE SLICES

INGREDIENTS

3 rolls prepackaged pie crust

½ cup cream cheese

1 cup goat cheese

1 cup heavy cream (or milk)

10 eggs

1 pound spinach, cooked and drained

1 pound kale, cooked and drained

2 cups Swiss Cheese, grated

1 cup Cheddar cheese, grated

1 ½ cup Parmesan cheese, grated

one bunch scallions, sliced thin

1 teaspoon salt

½ teaspoon pepper

EQUIPMENT

mixer and bowl

paper towels for draining greens

cheese grater or food processor

fork

12" x 18" sheet pan

parchment

measuring cups (1 cup, ½ cup)

measuring spoons (1 teaspoon, ½ teaspoon)

Preheat oven to 350°F.

Roll out crust dough and trim edges to make squares. Patch together square pieces to create rectangle about 15" x 22". Carefully transfer dough to sheet pan and gently press it into the corners.

Wrap excess dough into the pan so that the sides are slightly higher than the pan itself.

Bake for 10 minutes.

Remove from oven and cool.

Beat cream cheese and goat cheese together until slightly fluffy. Add eggs one at a time, beating to incorporate. Add cream and beat until slightly thick but not whipped. Add cheeses, scallions, greens, salt and pepper. Using a fork, stir to distribute ingredients evenly.

Pour into cooled crust. Gently level the filling so there are no watery patches.

Bake for 25 minutes.

Quiche will be puffed up until it cools.

Once cooled, cut into squares.

Serve warm or refrigerate. Keeps well for several days in fridge.

This is a great party dish that keeps well. The crust is optional.

Portable Chicken

SERVES 4-6

INGREDIENTS

5 pounds chicken thighs and/or drumsticks

2 Tablespoons salt

3 Tablespoons brown sugar

2 Tablespoons chili powder

2 Tablespoons paprika

2 teaspoons pepper

¼–½ teaspoon cayenne

EQUIPMENT

chef's knife and cutting board

dredging plate or bowl

wire rack

rimmed baking pan

toothpicks

roasting pan

measuring spoons (1 Tablespoon, 1 teaspoon, ½ teaspoon, ¼ teaspoon)

Use a sharp knife to make shallow slashes in the skin of the chicken, maybe 2-3 slashes per piece. Don't cut into the meat.

Mix spices together, then roll each thigh in the spice mixture. Make sure to cover the skin evenly all around.

Place the thighs on a wire rack over a rimmed cookie sheet. Refrigerate coated chicken for 6–24 hours to let flavors sink in.

Before cooking, poke toothpicks into skin to hold skin on to meat. (It will shrink and slide off the meat while cooking if you don't do this.)

Heat oven to 425°F. Roast chicken about 15-20 minutes. Raise heat to 500°F and cook for additional 5-8 minutes until no longer pink inside.

Let cool completely before serving, then wrap it up and take it on a picnic!

We took this chicken to the South Hero Fourth of July parade and ate it cold while everyone else waited for their lunch in long lines at Seb's. This recipe travels well and keeps for up to 4 days in the fridge.

Vegetable Lasagne

SERVES 8-10

INGREDIENTS

1 large can (28 ounces) diced tomatoes (basil added, if available)

2 Tablespoons olive oil

2 cloves garlic, minced

1 teaspoon salt

pinch red pepper flakes

2 cups Parmesan cheese, grated

1 cup ricotta or cottage cheese

1 cup heavy cream

2 cloves garlic, minced

1 teaspoon cornstarch

¼ teaspoon salt

¼ teaspoon pepper

1½ pounds eggplant, peeled and cut into ½" cubes (about 7 cups)

1 pound zucchini, cut into ½" pieces (about 4 cups)

1 pound yellow squash, cut into ½" pieces (about 4 cups)

5 Tablespoons plus 1 teaspoon olive oil

4 cloves garlic, minced

12 ounces spinach (about 12 cups)

12 no-boil lasagna noodles

½ cup Kalamata olives, chopped

12 ounces mozzarella, shredded (about 3 cups)

2 Tablespoons fresh basil, chopped

vegetable oil spray

Preheat oven to 375°F.

Whisk the first 5 ingredients together in bowl; set aside for the sauce. Whisk the next 7 ingredients together in bowl; set aside for the filling.

Toss eggplant with 1 teaspoon salt in large bowl. Line surface of large plate with paper towels and spray with vegetable oil spray. Spread eggplant in even layer over paper towels. Microwave eggplant, uncovered, until dry to touch and slightly shriveled, about 10 minutes, turning once halfway through to ensure that eggplant cooks evenly. Let cool slightly. Return eggplant to large bowl and toss with zucchini and squash.

Combine 1 Tablespoon oil and garlic in small bowl. Heat 2 Tablespoons oil in skillet over medium-high heat until shimmering. Add half eggplant mixture, ¼ teaspoon salt, and ¼ teaspoon pepper; cook, stirring occasionally, until vegetables are lightly browned, about 7 minutes. Push vegetables to sides of skillet; add half of garlic mixture to clearing and cook, mashing with spatula, until fragrant, about 30 seconds. Stir to combine garlic mixture with vegetables and transfer to medium bowl. Repeat with remaining eggplant mixture, 2 Tablespoons oil, and remaining garlic mixture.

Return skillet to medium-high heat, add remaining teaspoon oil, and heat until shimmering. Add spinach and cook, stirring frequently, until wilted, about 3 minutes. Transfer spinach to paper towel–lined plate and drain 2 minutes. Stir into eggplant mixture.

Spray 13" x 9" baking dish with vegetable oil spray. Spread 1 cup tomato sauce in bottom of baking dish; shingle 4 noodles on top of sauce. Spread half of vegetable mixture over noodles, followed by half of olives, half of filling mixture, and 1 cup of mozzarella. Repeat layering with 4 noodles, 1 cup tomato sauce, remaining vegetables, remaining olives, remaining filling mixture and 1 cup mozzarella. Place remaining 4 noodles on top layer of cheese. Spread remaining 1 cup tomato sauce over noodles and sprinkle with remaining 1 cup mozzarella. Lightly spray large sheet of aluminum foil with vegetable oil spray and cover lasagna. Bake until bubbling, about 35 minutes. Cool on wire rack 25 minutes. Cut into pieces, sprinkle with basil, and serve.

Back when we had a few vegetarians in the family, I collected recipes that were hearty enough so everyone could enjoy them. The trick is to drain the water out of the vegetables as much as possible before cooking so the lasagna is not watery. Yuck. If you're not a vegetarian, skip the eggplant, squash and zucchini and add some damn sausage.

EQUIPMENT

measuring spoons (1 Tablespoon, 1 teaspoon, ¼ teaspoon)

measuring cups (1 cup, ½ cup)

2 quart-sized bowls, 1 for filling and 1 for sauce

large bowl for tossing eggplant with salt

large plate for microwaving eggplant

whisk

paper towels

skillet

spatula

13" x 9" baking disk

aluminum foil

SWEETS

Almond Thumbprint Cookies

MAKES 12 COOKIES

INGREDIENTS

7 ounce box of Odense Almond Paste

¾ cup confectioner's sugar

1 Tablespoon plus 2 teaspoons flour

1 egg, separated (room temperature)

½ cup raspberry or apricot jam

1 cup thinly sliced almonds

EQUIPMENT

cookie sheet or sheet pan

parchment or wax paper

brush

egg separator

food processor

measuring cups (1 cup, ¾ cup, ½ cup)

measuring spoons (1 Tablespoon, 1 teaspoon)

mixing bowl

wire rack

Preheat oven to 350°F. Line cookie sheet with parchment.

Using a food processor or mixer, pulse almond paste and sugar until they are the texture of fine crumbs. Add flour and egg white, reserving yolk.

Mix until dough becomes a smooth paste, it will be slightly sticky. Turn dough out onto a lightly floured surface. With floured hands roll dough into a 12" log. Chill the dough if it is too warm to cut, and divide into 12 equal pieces.

Roll pieces into balls and place them 2" apart on a parchment-lined cookie sheet.

Flatten balls slightly into disks about ½" high.

Beat reserved egg yolk with 2 Tablespoons of water. Gently brush sides of disks with beaten yolk.

Press almonds into sides of disks then brush almonds lightly with egg wash, avoiding tops.

With your thumb, make an indentation in the center of each cookie. Fill centers with jam.

Bake 14 minutes or until light golden in color.

Gently pull parchment off cookies and cool them on wire rack.

Store cookies between sheets of wax paper in an airtight container.

These cookies taste insanely good. They have a crunchy outside texture balanced by the smooth almond inside. It should take you about 30 minutes to form the cookies and press almonds into the dough. Be patient! These make a nice complement to traditional Christmas cut-out cookies. Go easy on the jam before baking.

Apple Pie

SERVES 8

INGREDIENTS

6 large Granny Smith apples (any kind will do in a pinch)

5 Tablespoons sugar

2 Tablespoons Instant Clear Jel or cornstarch

1 teaspoons cinnamon

1 Tablespoon lemon juice

2 Tablespoons butter

double pie crust

1 egg yolk, whisked with 1 Tablespoon water

EQUIPMENT

measuring spoons (1 Tablespoon, 1 teaspoon)

pie plate

apple corer, peeler

chef's knife and cutting board

pastry brush

Preheat oven to 350°F.

Form a single layer of pie crust over a pie plate, prick the bottom lightly with a fork and bake for 10 minutes or until golden brown. Cool.

Core, peel and slice the apples.

Toss the apples in a bowl with the sugar, Clear-Jel, cinnamon and lemon juice and microwave them for 6 minutes.

Strain the juice and put aside. Scoop the apple slices into the pie crust, pressing down to flatten them.

Microwave juice until ¼ cup remains then pour over the apples.

Lay the second crust over the top of the apples, gently folding the dough under the bottom crust.

Brush with egg wash and make a few fork holes in the top crust.

Bake for 30 minutes.

Note: To make lattice crust, roll out dough onto a piece of parchment and cut with a chef's knife into at least 12 half inch strips. Refrigerate the dough for 30 minutes so it's pliable but not hard. Lay the first two strips perpendicular to each other at the edge of the pie. Lay the next two strips, folding back every other horizontal strip before you lay the next vertical one. Fold the ends neatly under the bottom crust. Brush with egg wash.

Apple pie doesn't need a special occasion. It doesn't need Fall. It doesn't need Thanksgiving. You don't need an excuse to make this any time you feel like it. This recipe eliminates one of my pet peeves – watery apple goo on the bottom of the pie crust – by pre-cooking the apples so excessive juice never makes it to the pie. The pie will be plenty moist without it.

No one loves making or eating homemade crust more than I do, but you won't regret using store-bought crust or a crust mix.

Chocolate Sugar-Dusted Cookies

SERVES 4-6

INGREDIENTS

1 cup flour

½ cup unsweetened cocoa powder

1 teaspoon baking powder

¼ teaspoon baking soda

½ teaspoon salt

1½ cups brown sugar, packed

3 large eggs

4 teaspoons instant coffee (or Starbucks Via package)

1 teaspoon vanilla

4 ounces unsweetened chocolate, chopped

4 Tablespoons unsalted butter

1 cup granulated sugar

1 cup confectioner's sugar

EQUIPMENT

measuring cups
(1 cup, ½ cup)

measuring spoons
(1 Tablespoon, 1 teaspoon, ½ teaspoon, ¼ teaspoon)

5 bowls:
1 large
2 quart-sized
2 shallow pint-sized bowls

whisk

mixer

small ice cream scoop or large tablespoon

parchment

2 baking sheets

Preheat oven to 325°F.

Line 2 baking sheets with parchment paper.

Whisk flour, cocoa, baking powder, baking soda, and salt together in your primary, large bowl.

Whisk brown sugar; eggs; coffee powder and vanilla in a slightly smaller bowl.

Combine chocolate and butter in a quart-sized bowl and microwave for 90 seconds.

Whisk chocolate mixture and egg mixture into flour mixture and mix thoroughly.

Let dough sit at room temperature for a few minutes.

Place granulated sugar and confectioner's sugar in separate shallow dishes.

Use a small ice cream scoop to roll the dough into balls.

Drop dough balls directly into granulated sugar and roll or use a spoon to coat.

Transfer dough balls to confectioner's sugar and roll to coat evenly. Space dough balls 2" apart on prepared sheets.

Bake cookies, 1 sheet at a time, until puffed and cracked and edges have begun to set but centers are still soft (cookies will look raw between cracks and seem underdone), about 12 minutes, rotating sheet halfway through baking.

Let cool completely on sheet before serving.

Expect to mess up several bowls when you make these impressive looking cookies. It's worth it.

Chocolate Raspberry Cheesecake Brownies

MAKES 16 SQUARES

INGREDIENTS

1 (8 ounce) package cream cheese, softened to room temperature

1½ cup sugar

1 large egg yolk

2¼ teaspoon vanilla

⅔ cup flour

½ teaspoon baking powder

½ teaspoon salt

¼ pound (1 stick) unsalted butter

4 ounces unsweetened chocolate, chopped

½ cup raspberry jam

3 large eggs

vegetable oil spray

EQUIPMENT

measuring cups (1 cup, ⅓ cup, ½ cup)

measuring spoons (1 teaspoon, ½ teaspoon, ¼ teaspoon)

food processor

8" square pan

foil

whisk

toothpick

rubber spatula

Preheat oven to 350°F.

Line 8" square pan with foil and coat with vegetable oil spray. Leave some foil hanging over the edge of the pan so you can pull the brownies out when they are done.

Process cream cheese, ¼ cup of the sugar, egg yolk and ¾ teaspoon of the vanilla in food processor until smooth.

Combine flour, baking powder and salt in a bowl.

Microwave butter and chocolate in a large bowl for about a minute.

Whisk in ¼ cup jam and cool slightly.

Add remaining 1¼ cup sugar, eggs and remaining 1½ teaspoon vanilla to chocolate mixture, stirring until combined.

Add flour mixture and stir until incorporated.

Microwave remaining jam about 30 seconds and stir. Scrape half of batter into prepared pan.

Dollop cream cheese filling over batter and spread into even layer.

Dollop warm jam over filling and swirl to partially combine. Spread remaining batter evenly over filling.

Bake until toothpick inserted in center comes out with a few crumbs attached, about 60 minutes.

Cool 2 hours.

Using foil, lift brownies from pan and cut into squares.

I made these for Christmas gifts in 2010. They used to be Maisie's favorite.

Chocolate Stout Cake

MAKES A DOUBLE LAYER ROUND CAKE

INGREDIENTS

Cake

2 cups stout or dark beer, such as Guinness

2 cups (4 sticks) unsalted butter

1½ cups dark cocoa

4 cups flour

4 cups sugar

1 Tablespoon baking powder

1½ teaspoons salt

4 large eggs

¾ cup sour cream

oil or spray for greasing pans

Frosting

1 pound bittersweet or semisweet chocolate, chopped

2 cups heavy cream

1 teaspoon vanilla

vegetable oil spray

EQUIPMENT

measuring cups (1 cup, ½ cup, ¼ cup)

measuring spoons (1 Tablespoon, 1 teaspoon, ½ teaspoon)

medium saucepan

medium mixing bowl

electric mixer

large bowl

whisk

metal spoon

cake plate

parchment paper

pencil & scissors

three 8" or two 9" cake pans

toothpicks or cake tester

Preheat the oven to 350°F.

Coat three 8" or two 9" cake pans with vegetable oil spray, and line them with parchment paper circles.

Place the stout and butter in a saucepan, and heat until the butter melts. Remove the pan from the heat, and add the cocoa powder. Whisk until the mixture is smooth. Set aside to cool to room temperature.

Whisk together the flour, sugar, baking powder, and salt in a medium bowl and set aside. In a larger mixing bowl, beat together the eggs and sour cream and mix in the stout-cocoa mixture. Add the flour mixture and mix together at slow speed for at least a minute, scraping down the sides. Divide the batter equally by weight between the two (or three) pans.

Bake the layers for 35 minutes for 8" pans, or 45-50 minutes for 9" pans, until a toothpick inserted into the center comes out clean. Remove the cakes from the oven and cool on a rack for 10 minutes before turning the cakes out of their pans. Return to the rack to finish cooling completely before frosting.

For the frosting, place the chopped chocolate in a large heatproof bowl. Bring the cream to a simmer in a saucepan. Pour the hot cream over the chocolate and stir with a metal spoon until the mixture is completely smooth. Stir in the vanilla. Refrigerate until the icing is spreadable, stirring occasionally, about 2 hours.

Trim both cake layers to have a flat top so they layers won't crack when you place them upside down on your cake plate.

Line the edges of a cake plate with parchment, and then place the layer upside down on top. Spread ⅔ cup of the icing over just the top of the layer.

Top with another cake layer, top side down, and repeat the process. If you baked three layers, add that one also. Use the remaining frosting to cover the top and sides of the cake. Remove the parchment.

When a recipe starts with a pound of butter, a bottle of beer and four cups of sugar, you know it's going to taste great. The batter is dark and richly flavored.

If you're tempted to use a cake mix, don't do it! This recipe makes an unbelievably good cake without much work. The cake comes out perfectly every time.

Dewar's Apple Cake

SERVES 10

INGREDIENTS

Cake

2 medium apples peeled, cored and quartered (or 1 cup applesauce)

1½ sticks butter (¾ cup), softened

1½ cups sugar

1 teaspoon cinnamon

4 eggs

2½ cups flour

2 teaspoons baking powder

½ teaspoon salt

½ cup Dewar's or other whiskey

oil and flour for the pan

Glaze

1 cup dark brown sugar

¼ cup butter

¼ cup heavy cream

1 cup confectioner's sugar

1 Tablespoon Dewar's

EQUIPMENT

9" Bundt pan

cake plate

parchment paper

whisk

food processor

apple corer

apple peeler

measuring cups (1 cup, ½ cup, ¼ cup)

measuring spoons (1 Tablespoon, 1 teaspoon, ½ teaspoon)

rubber spatula

Preheat the oven to 350°F.

Oil and flour the bundt pan.

Put apples in a food processor and pulse until they are the size of the crunched up potato chips at the bottom of the bag; remove the apples from the processor bowl and set aside.

In the processor, combine 1½ sticks butter with 1½ cups sugar and pulse until combined. With motor running, add eggs one at a time. Add apple purée and process until just combined.

In a large bowl, whisk together flour, baking powder, cinnamon and salt. Add about a third of the flour mixture to apple mixture in the food processor. Then, with motor running, add ¼ cup of Dewar's; add another third of the flour, followed by remaining ¼ cup of Dewar's, then finally, the last of the flour. Process until batter is smooth.

Using rubber spatula, scrape batter into prepared pan and bake until the middle is set (your fingers should leave only a small indentation when you gently press cake), 45-50 minutes. When done, cool in pan for about 10 minutes.

For the glaze, combine the brown sugar, butter and heavy cream in a small saucepan. Bring to a boil and cook, without stirring, for 1 minute. Stir down the glaze and remove from heat. Whisk in confectioner's sugar and Dewar's.

When cake is completely cooled, at least an hour after baking, invert the pan onto a very flat cake plate lined with parchment.

Drizzle glaze over the cake evenly.

Let glaze cool until it is hardened. Once hardened, remove parchment.

This cake is completely foolproof. There's no luck required. You can substitute any hard liquor for the whiskey. Try this with Appalachian Gap coffee liqueur. The apple and coffee combination make it brunch-like, the apple and scotch combination is more dinner-like.

Fig Cookies

MAKES 12-15 COOKIES

INGREDIENTS

2 cups of dried figs, stems removed, chopped

¾ cup maple syrup

a squirt of lemon juice

1 cup sifted white flour

2 cups sifted whole wheat flour

1 teaspoon baking powder

½ teaspoon baking soda

½ teaspoon salt

¼ pound (1 stick) butter, room temperature

½ cup light brown sugar, firmly packed

½ cup honey

1 egg

1 cup confectioner's sugar and 1 Tablespoon water

EQUIPMENT

measuring cups (1 cup, ½ cup)

measuring spoons (1 teaspoon, ½ teaspoon)

mixer

small saucepan

cookie sheet

parchment

rolling pin

Preheat the oven to 350°F.

For the filling, cook the dried fruit in a saucepan with the syrup and the lemon juice until soft.

For the cookie dough, whisk the flours, baking powder, baking soda and salt together.

Cream the butter with an electric mixer.

Add sugar and beat well.

Beat in honey and egg.

Gradually add the flour mixture.

Beat until completely mixed.

Turn dough out onto parchment paper. Flatten slightly and refrigerate 30 minutes. Once chilled, roll dough into a 15"x 6" rectangle.

Spread the fig filling in a 2" strip in the middle of the dough. Fold dough in thirds so that one 15" side overlaps the fig filling and the other 15" side lies on top of that.

Place dough on a cookie sheet seam side down.

Bake at 350°F for 15 minutes, then flip the dough and bake it another 10 minutes.

Cool cookies on a rack.

To frost, combine confectioner's sugar and water and drizzle on cooled cookies.

Cut into rectangles.

I had some dried figs left over after Christmas and scouted for a way to use them. This recipe is a mash up of Flour: A Baker's Collection of Spectacular Recipes *by Joanne Chang and* Maida Heatter's Book of Great Cookies *by Maida Heatter. If you like Fig Newtons even a little bit, you will find these addicting.*

Lemon Layer Cake

SERVES 12

INGREDIENTS

Cake

2½ cups cake flour

½ teaspoon baking powder

½ teaspoon baking soda

¼ teaspoon salt

1 cup (2 sticks) unsalted butter, slightly softened

1½ cups granulated sugar

2 whole eggs, room temperature

3 egg yolks, room temperature

2 teaspoons vanilla extract

1 teaspoon grated lemon zest

¼ cup fresh lemon juice

½ cup whole milk

Filling

2 large egg yolks

⅓ cup granulated sugar

¼ cup fresh lemon juice

2 Tablespoons unsalted butter, slightly softened

pinch of salt

1 teaspoon finely grated lemon zest

½ cup heavy cream

Frosting

¾ cup (1½ sticks) unsalted butter, softened

3½ cups confectioner's sugar

2 Tablespoons heavy cream

2 teaspoons fresh lemon juice

¼ teaspoon vanilla extract

1 teaspoon finely grated lemon zest

Preheat the oven to 350°F.

Butter and flour the bottom and sides of two 8" cake pans.

Whisk together the flour, baking powder, baking soda, and salt in a small bowl and set aside.

Beat the butter until creamy. Add the sugar and continue to beat until the mixture is light. Add the whole eggs and egg yolks, one at a time, beating well after each addition. Beat in the vanilla and lemon zest. Gradually beat in the lemon juice (the batter will appear curdled at this point, but will smooth out after you add the dry ingredients). Beat in the dry ingredients in 3 additions alternately with milk in 2 additions. Scrape down the sides of the bowl and beat for another 10 seconds. Scrape the batter into the pans, weighing to make sure they have the same volume.

Bake the layers for 25 minutes, or until a toothpick inserted into the center of each one comes out clean. Cool the cakes until warm, then invert them onto racks until completely cool.

For the filling, whisk the yolks and sugar in a small saucepan. Whisk in the lemon juice, butter, and salt. Cook over medium-low heat, stirring gently until the mixture turns opaque, about 3 minutes.

Pour the mixture through a strainer into a little bowl. Stir in the lemon zest and allow to cool.

Cover with plastic wrap, pressing directly onto the surface, and refrigerate for 1 hour.

Beat the heavy cream on high speed until soft peaks form. Gently fold lemon filling into whipped cream. Cover and refrigerate.

For the frosting, beat the butter until creamy. Beat in the confectioner's sugar. Add the cream, lemon juice, vanilla, and lemon zest and beat until fluffy.

Cover bottom layer with filling. Pipe a ring of frosting on top as a "gate" to hold in the filling. Add filling and top layer and cover top and sides with frosting.

Between Paul's birthday on June 19th, Dad's on the 21st, Maisie's on the 24th and Rhiannnon's on the 26th, June at Bayviews has seen some serious cake madness. Although this recipe requires time, it stands out for its flavor. To save time, grate the lemon peel, juice the lemons, measure out the butter, cream and eggs before you start.

EQUIPMENT

measuring cups (1 cup, ½ cup, ⅓ cup, ¼ cup)

measuring spoons (1 Tablespoon, 1 teaspoon, ½ teaspoon, ¼ teaspoon)

whisk

egg separator

rubber spatula

mixer

lemon grater

lemon juicer

small bowl for mixing dry ingredients

large mixing bowl for cake batter

2 8" cake pans

toothpick

medium non-aluminum sauce pan

strainer

medium bowl for whipping cream

small bowl for lemon curd

medium bowl for frosting

cooling rack

Peanut Butter & Jelly Swirl Blondies

MAKES 9 PIECES

INGREDIENTS

2½ cups flour

½ teaspoon salt

½ teaspoon baking soda

12 Tablespoons unsalted butter, melted and cooled

1 cup brown sugar, packed

2 teaspoons vanilla extract

1 egg, room temperature

1 egg yolk, at room temperature

5 dollops creamy peanut butter

4 dollops raspberry or strawberry jam

EQUIPMENT

8" x 8" baking pan

measuring cups
(1 cup, ½ cup, ⅓ cup)

measuring spoons
(1 Tablespoon, 1 teaspoon, ½ teaspoon, ⅛ teaspoon)

mixer and bowl

rubber spatula

large spoon for making dollops

knife to swirl peanut butter with jam

knife to cut blondies

Preheat the oven to 325°F.

Line an 8" square pan with foil. Whisk the flour, salt and baking soda in a bowl. Set aside.

Mix together the melted butter, brown sugar and vanilla extract. Add in the egg and the egg yolk and mix well.

Slowly add in the dry ingredients and mix until almost combined. Use a rubber spatula to fold the ingredients all together.

Spread the batter out into the pan. Place dollops of the peanut butter and dollops of the jam in a checkerboard pattern on top of the batter.

Swirl the peanut butter and jam throughout the top of the blondie batter, just gently. The mixture should retain its distinct parts. Bake at 325°F for 25 minutes. Cool completely on a rack and cut into 9 pieces.

A serious indulgence that combines the taste of your childhood lunch with an uptown salted caramel vibe. If you cut these right, everyone gets a square with both a crunchy edge and a creamy corner, except for the dense, rich middle square which gets saved for the middle child.

Popcorn Balls from Cranny

MAKES MANY!

INGREDIENTS

2 cups sugar

1 package microwave popcorn

EQUIPMENT

measuring cups (1 cup)

microwave

rimmed baking pan

sauce pan

metal spoon

Pop the corn. Spread it on a baking pan. Throw away all the unpopped kernels. (If we'd had vegetable oil spray, I'd have coated the pan first.)

Heat the sugar in a heavy sauce pan until it turns pumpkin orange, stirring constantly. When it is syrupy and golden, pour it evenly over the popcorn.

Quickly stir the popcorn with a spoon so most of it gets some caramel. (I'd have used an ice cream scoop if I'd had one.) The sugar will be incredibly hot and can burn you terribly, so do this carefully. Precision doesn't matter.

How many times did we drive hours to get to South Hero, eating fast food along the way only to find when we got there the cupboards were bare. One time, after we arrived, Maisie was so sad that there was nothing to eat. I tried to convince her that, even with the meagre staples left in the cupboard over the winter, we still could cook up something delicious. Here is the result.

Terry Delano's Hot Fudge Sauce

MAKES 4 PINTS

INGREDIENTS

1½ cups white sugar

1 cup light brown sugar, packed

2 cups dark cocoa, unsweetened

1 cup unsalted butter (two sticks) cut into small pieces

2 cups heavy cream

1 teaspoon vanilla

¼ teaspoon salt (Terry uses kosher salt)

EQUIPMENT

measuring cups (1 cup, ½ cup)

measuring spoons (1 teaspoon, ¼ teaspoon)

double boiler or metal bowl that fits snugly into a saucepan

whisk or metal spoon

4 pint glass jars with lids

Mix the sugars together in the top of a double boiler. Use your fingers to press all the lumps apart into granules. When all lumps are gone, add the cocoa and mix well.

Put the bowl over a pan filled about ⅓ way up with boiling water at medium heat.

Add the cream and the butter. Mix really well. All the sugar crystals should dissolve. This should take about 5 minutes.

Remove from heat.

Add vanilla and mix well. Let the sauce rest about 5 minutes.

Pour carefully into glass jars with lids. Cool and store in fridge.

Once, I knocked on Terry's door to say hello around Christmas time hoping he'd offer me a jar of his hot fudge sauce. The year I moved to Vermont, he gave me the recipe. That was around the time Phoebe started serving it at the Paddle, so now you can either make it or order it. This makes a great gift, but if you don't have any friends, it can stay in the fridge for months. Terry admits he stole this recipe from the naptime chef, Kelsey Banfield who admits she stole it from Rhoda Janis.

Applejack Bars

MAKES 16 SQUARES

INGREDIENTS

1½ cups flour

1 teaspoon baking powder

¼ teaspoon baking soda

1 teaspoon cinnamon

1 teaspoon cardamom

1 cup brown sugar

8 Tablespoons salted butter, melted and cooled

2 eggs, lightly beaten

½ cup applesauce

1 teaspoon vanilla

1 Tablespoon applejack or whiskey (optional)

1 apple, peeled and chopped

½ cup chopped walnuts and/or dried cranberries (optional)

2½ Tablespoons heavy cream

⅓ cup brown sugar

2½ Tablespoons butter

1 teaspoon maple syrup

½ teaspoon vanilla

vegetable oil spray

EQUIPMENT

8" square baking pan

measuring cups (1 cup, ½ cup, ⅓ cup)

measuring spoons (1 Tablespoon, 1 teaspoon, ½ teaspoon, ¼ teaspoon)

whisk

medium bowl for flour mixture

quart-sized saucepan for wet ingredients and glaze

rubber spatula

toothpicks

wire rack

Preheat the oven to 350°F.

Coat an 8" square baking pan with vegetable oil spray and flour.

Whisk flour, baking powder, baking soda and spices in medium bowl and set aside. Whisk brown sugar into the melted butter. Whisk in eggs, mixing until well-blended. Add applesauce, vanilla and applejack and whisk until smooth.

Stir in dry ingredients, chopped apple and walnuts/dried cranberries. Don't overmix.

Turn batter into prepared pan, smoothing top with rubber spatula.

Bake until toothpick inserted in center of cake comes out clean, 20-25 minutes.

Cool on wire rack.

Bring cream, brown sugar, butter and maple syrup to a boil, whisking attentively. Adjust heat and simmer 5 minutes.

Add vanilla.

Pour hot glaze over cooled bars.

Serve when cooled.

These were a favorite in your school days. The whiskey helped me do your homework. Adapted from Baking – From My Home to Yours *by Dorie Greenspan.*

Butterscotch Candy

SERVES 6

INGREDIENTS

½ cup brown sugar
¼ cup butter
½ cup white sugar
½ cup water
2 teaspoons vinegar
1 pinch salt
½ teaspoon vanilla
vegetable oil spray

EQUIPMENT

measuring cups
(½ cup, ¼ cup)

measuring spoons
(1 teaspoon, ½ teaspoon)

foil

medium saucepan with lid

loaf pan

candy thermometer or
small bowl of cold water

table knife

Coat loaf pan with vegetable oil spray.

In a medium saucepan over medium heat, combine brown sugar, butter, white sugar, water, vinegar and salt. Cover and bring to a boil.

Remove lid and heat, without stirring, to 270°F–290°F or until a small amount of syrup dropped into cold water forms hard but pliable threads.

Pour in vanilla, but do not stir.

Remove from heat and pour into prepared pan.

Let cool slightly before cutting into squares and allowing candy to cool completely.

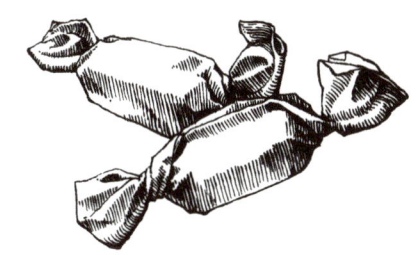

My notes on this recipe say "Save this one. Best ever."

Carrot Cake

SERVES 8

INGREDIENTS

Cake

2½ cups flour

1¼ teaspoon baking powder

1 teaspoon baking soda

2 teaspoons cinnamon

½ teaspoon salt

1½ cups sugar

½ cup light brown sugar (packed)

4 large eggs

1 cup oil

6 medium carrots, shredded

1½ cups walnuts, chopped (optional)

vegetable oil spray

Frosting

8 ounces cream cheese

5 Tablespoons unsalted butter

1 Tablespoon sour cream

½ teaspoon vanilla

1 cup confectioner's sugar

EQUIPMENT

measuring cups (1 cup, ½ cup)

measuring spoons (1 Tablespoon, 1 teaspoon, ½teaspoon, ¼teaspoon)

13"x 9" baking pan or two 8" round pans

parchment

whisk

mixer and bowl for sugar, eggs and oil

large mixing bowl for dry ingredients

rubber spatula

toothpicks

Preheat the oven to 350°F.

Coat a 13" x 9" pan or two 8" round pans with vegetable oil spray and line with parchment.

Whisk flour, baking powder, baking soda, cinnamon and salt in large bowl. Set aside.

Beat sugars and eggs until frothy.

Add oil and beat until batter is well-emulsified.

Scrape wet ingredients into dry ones and add carrots and 1 cup walnuts.

Mix just until combined.

Pour into prepared pan(s).

Bake until a toothpick comes out clean, about 35-40 minutes. Cool.

For the frosting, mix cream cheese, butter, sour cream, vanilla and confectioner's sugar.

Fill layers and coat outside of cake with frosting.

Garnish sides or top border with ½ cup chopped walnuts.

Charlie requests this cake every August 6th.

St. George's Day Cookie Bars

MAKES 36 BARS

INGREDIENTS

1 cup pecans

1½ cups unsweetened coconut

1½ cup flour

1 teaspoon baking powder

½ teaspoon salt

1½ sticks unsalted butter, melted

1½ cups light brown sugar

2 large eggs

4 teaspoons vanilla

6 ounces white chocolate chips or half chocolate and half white

vegetable oil spray

EQUIPMENT

measuring cups (1 cup, ½ cup)

measuring spoons (1 teaspoon, ½ teaspoon)

rimmed baking sheet

chef's knife and cutting board

parchment

whisk

medium bowl for dry ingredients

medium bowl for butter and sugar

rubber spatula

wire rack

Preheat the oven to 350°F.

Spread nuts on large rimmed baking sheet and bake 7 minutes.

Transfer nuts to cutting board. Cool; chop and set aside.

Toast coconut on same rimmed baking sheet, stirring 2 to 3 times, until light golden, about 3 minutes.

Cut 18"x 8" piece of parchment and fit into 13"x 9" baking pan, allowing excess to overhang pan edges. Cut 12" by 8" piece of parchment and fit into width of baking pan in same manner,

Spray with vegetable oil spray.

Whisk flour, baking powder, and salt together in a medium bowl; set aside.

Whisk melted butter and brown sugar together in medium bowl until combined.

Add eggs and vanilla and mix well. Using rubber spatula, fold dry ingredients into egg mixture until just combined; do not overmix.

Fold in chocolate, coconut, and nuts and turn batter into pan, smoothing top.

Bake until top is shiny, cracked, and light golden brown, 22-25 minutes. Do not overbake.

Cool on wire rack.

Remove bars from pan by lifting parchment overhang and transfer to cutting board.

Cut into 2-inch squares and serve.

At one time these were Maisie's favorite. We submitted a recipe like this to the St. Peter's cookbook.

BREAD

Baguettes

MAKES 4 BAGUETTES

INGREDIENTS

8 cups flour

1 Tablespoon table salt or 1½ Tablespoons kosher salt

1 Tablespoon yeast

3 cups lukewarm water

vegetable oil spray

EQUIPMENT

6 quart large bowl or small bucket with cover

1 quart glass measuring bowl

measuring cups (1 cup)

measuring spoons (1 Tablespoon)

whisk

baking pan

knife to slash loaf before baking

spray bottle for spritzing loaf with water (optional)

Whisk the dry ingredients in the bowl and pour in the water. Mix with your hands until there are no dry spots, then knead the dough gently on the counter for a few minutes.

Wash and dry the bowl, then lightly coat it with vegetable oil spray.

Plop in the dough, cover the bowl and let rest at room temperature for 2 hours.

Refrigerate overnight, or for up to 7 days.

To bake the bread: Scoop out about ¼ of the dough. Place dough on a lightly greased work surface. Shape the dough into a rough, slightly flattened oval.

Fold the dough in half lengthwise, and seal the edges with the heel of your hand. Flatten slightly, and fold lengthwise and seal again.

Gently roll the of dough into a 15" log.

Place the log seam-side down onto a lightly greased or parchment-lined baking sheet, or into the well of a baguette pan.

Cover and allow the dough to rise till it's very puffy, about 1½ hours. Towards the end of the rising time, preheat your oven to 450°F.

Slash the baguette and spritz it heavily with warm water.

Bake until deep golden brown, 25-30 minutes.

Remove from the oven and cool on a rack.

Okay, so there is a little kneading. You can do this. Really. King Arthur Flour originated this recipe, but it's been in The New York Times, *too.*

87

Banana Bread

SERVES 12

INGREDIENTS

1 ¾ cups flour

1 teaspoon baking soda

½ teaspoon salt

½ cup butter, unsalted

5 frozen and 1 fresh(er) banana

2 large eggs

1 cup dark brown sugar, packed

1 teaspoon cinnamon

1 teaspoon vanilla

¾ cup chopped walnuts

2 teaspoons granulated sugar

vegetable oil spray

EQUIPMENT

loaf pan

measuring cups (1 cup, ¼ cup)

measuring spoons (1 teaspoon, ½ teaspoon)

2 small glass bowls

quart size glass bowl

larger mixing bowl

small strainer

Preheat the oven to 350°F.

Coat a 8 ½" x 4 ½" loaf pan with vegetable oil spray.

Mix flour, baking soda and salt in a small bowl.

In a separate glass bowl, melt the butter and set aside to cool.

In a quart-size glass bowl, microwave the 5 frozen bananas for 2 minutes, checking so the juice doesn't boil over.

Strain the bananas and catch the juice into a smaller glass bowl. There should be about a cup of juice.

Microwave just the juice for about 4 minutes, or until there's only ¼ cup left.

Add the concentrated juice to the pulp and mash lightly.

Add the eggs, brown sugar, cinnamon and vanilla to the butter, stirring well.

Pour in the banana pulp. Add the flour mixture and walnuts and stir until just combined.

Pour the batter into the prepared pan.

Slice the 6th banana and arrange slices on top of the batter in two parallel lines of shingles. Sprinkle with granulated sugar.

Bake for 55-65 minutes or until a toothpick comes out clean.

The minute you feel the snap of Fall, it's time to make this recipe. Save aging bananas in a ziplock bag in the freezer. Once you have 5 or 6, plus one that you are still able to slice, you are ready to make this bread. Matt says the frozen banana pulp looks like brains, but I say it looks like Autumn.

SS France Croissants

YIELDS 24 CROISSANTS

INGREDIENTS

3 Tablespoons flour

3 sticks butter, room temperature,

4 cups flour

2 teaspoon salt

2 Tablespoons sugar

5 teaspoons dry yeast

¼ cup 85°-*ish* water

1½ cups 85°-*ish* milk

½ cup 85°-*ish* half-and-half

1 egg

1 Tablespoon water

EQUIPMENT

foil

rolling pin

gallon ziplock bag

kitchen towel

ruler

1 quart glass measuring bowl

measuring cups (1 cup)

measuring spoons (1 Tablespoon, 1 teaspoon)

instant read thermometer (optional)

stand mixer with dough hook (optional)

small bowl and pastry brush for egg wash

pizza cutter or knife

baking sheet

Sprinkle 3 Tablespoons flour over butter and blend with your hands until no traces of flour remain. On a length of foil, make a 6" square of the butter mixture and cover with more foil.

Place in the refrigerator for 2-3 hours.

In a large bowl, blend 2 cups flour with salt and sugar. Dissolve yeast in warm water and add it with the milk and half-and-half to the flour mixture.

Mix the batterlike dough with a mixer using a dough hook about 2 minutes. Stir in additional flour, ¼ cup at a time, to make a soft dough (it will stiffen when chilled.) Knead by hand or with the dough hook to form a solid mass.

Cover the bowl and refrigerate for at least 1 hour.

Bring the butter block to room temperature slowly. Ideally, the butter in the dough and the butter in the block should be about the same temperature; 65°F is ideal. The block of butter should bend but not break (too cold) nor be oily (too warm) when bent slightly.

Place the dough on a floured work surface and with your hands press it into a 10"square. Unwrap the block of butter and lay the block diagonally on the dough. Bring each point of dough into the center, overlapping the edges at least 1". Press the dough into a neat package.

With a heavy rolling pin, roll the dough into a rectangle, approximately 8"x 18" or 10"x 20".

Fold the length of dough into thirds, as for a letter. Turn so that the open ends are at twelve and six o'clock. Roll again into a rectangle. This time, fold both ends into the middle and then close, as one would a book.

Wrap the package of dough in a clean cloth that has been soaked in cold water and wrung dry. Place the wrapped dough in a gallon ziplock bag in the refrigerator for 1-2 hours.

Remove the dough from the refrigerator and place on a floured work surface. Unwrap, roll out, and fold in thirds, as for a letter. This is the final turn before it is rolled out and cut into croissants. Dampen cloth

These are unbelievably good. They look and taste like bakery croissants and are easier than making bread (very little kneading.) The recipe is from the kitchen of the SS France. Legend has it that steerage passengers just got rectangles, not lovely triangles rolled into crescents. Allow some time for the dough to progress, but there's not a huge time investment in this recipe.

again and wrap loosely around the dough. Place the package in the ziplock bag so moisture will be retained.

Leave in the refrigerator 4-6 hours or overnight.

Mix together the egg and 1 Tablespoon water. Have ready the egg wash, a knife or pizza cutter, and a ruler if you wish the pieces to be cut precisely otherwise, plan to cut them freehand. Sprinkle work surface with flour.

Roll the dough until it is a 10"x 35" rectangle, and, most importantly, about ¼" thick. This is a crucial dimension, since it determines the size and texture of the croissants. Trim irregularities to make the rectangle uniform. Cut the rectangle lengthwise to make two 5" pieces. Cut the strip into triangles, 5" wide on the bottom.

Separate the triangles, place them on a baking sheet, and chill for 15-20 minutes.

Roll the dough into the traditional croissant shape by rolling from the base to the point. Some bakers put a small notch in the base of the triangle to make it easier to pull the base wider as they roll.

Place the croissants on a baking sheet and allow to rise for 1-2 hours. they will double in volume.

Preheat the oven to 425°F. Brush the croissants with the egg wash.

Bake the croissants for 22-25 minutes. Allow them to cool on a rack before serving.

SIDES

Baked Apples

SERVES 4

INGREDIENTS

2-4 apples

3 Tablespoons maple syrup

Optional Ingredients

1 teaspoon cinnamon

2 Tablespoon dried cranberries

1 Tablespoon walnuts, chopped

EQUIPMENT

measuring spoons
(1 Tablespoon, 1 teaspoon)

chef's knife and cutting board

baking dish

Preheat oven to 350°F.

Core the apples and cut them in half along the equator.

Lay them cut side up in an oven-proof baking dish or a microwavable baking dish.

Pour syrup over the apples and sprinkle with cinnamon.

Bake, covered with foil, for 30 minutes.

Fill cores with chopped walnuts and cranberries and spoon melted syrup over the apples.

Return to oven, uncovered, for 10 minutes.

Matt likes this recipe. Nana made this as a standard supper side dish or a dessert. It's easy and it's a great way to use up aging apples.

Jalapeno Red Onion Relish

MAKES 10–12 SERVINGS

INGREDIENTS

3 cups water

1 cup apple cider vinegar

1 cup sugar

1 jalapeno pepper

3-4 red onions

EQUIPMENT

1 quart size (or larger) mason jar

sharp knife

cutting board

mandolin or slicer

measuring cups (1 cup)

Pour the water into a large mason jar and heat it for 2 minutes in the microwave. Add the vinegar and the sugar and stir.

Cut the jalapeno into 2 halves and remove the seeds using rubber gloves. Slice the pepper into about 60 very thin slices.

Add them to the jar.

To slice the onions, first cut off the stem and root ends (the poles,) then cut the onion in half (along the equator.) If you are using a mandolin to slice the onion, use the 3.0 mm setting. Thinner slices make the relish easier to use on burgers or as topping. Any thicker and the relish becomes a more dominant ingredient. It's hard to cut onion slices this thin with a knife.

Add the sliced onions to the jar.

Shake the jar to distribute the ingredients and refrigerate at least one day.

Relish will keep refrigerated for a couple of weeks.

We first saw this relish on the counter at El Encuentro de Centro Americano in Morristown. We loved how it accented the food. This recipe is my best guess at how they made it. If you care about the clarity of the liquid, try using plain white vinegar since the apple cider vinegar gives the mixture a brown tinge. Either way, this tastes great on burgers or alongside anything with beef.

Mahogany Baked Beans

SERVES MANY

INGREDIENTS

2 pounds dry great northern beans

2 cups molasses

½ cup brown sugar

1 Tablespoon dried mustard

½ pound raw bacon

3 beef bouillon cubes, crushed

1 teaspoon salt

1 teaspoon pepper

1 Tablespoon Dijon mustard

1 teaspoon onion powder

1 Tablespoon Worcestershire sauce

1 Tablespoon ketchup

lots of water

EQUIPMENT

measuring cups (1 cup, ½ cup)

measuring spoons (1 Tablespoon, 1 teaspoon)

Dutch oven

Preheat oven to 300°F.

Put the beans into a very large Dutch oven and cover with water. Bring to a boil.

Remove from heat and add 1 cup molasses, the brown sugar, the dried mustard, bacon, 2 crushed bouillon cubes, salt and pepper.

Stir. Cover and place in oven for 3 hours.

Uncover and stir.

Add the second cup of molasses, the Dijon mustard, onion powder, Worcestershire, ketchup and last crushed bouillon cube.

Add water if beans are not completely submerged.

Bake for an additional 3 hours, uncovered.

Stir occasionally while bean sauce thickens. If they are still too watery after 3 hours, bring them to the stove and cook over low heat until thickened. If they are not liquid enough, add water and return to oven to cook, uncovered, until sauce thickens.

This recipe is as much like canned beans as an Edwardian sideboard is like an Ikea coffee table. Both do their job well, but you can build your kitchen around this recipe. The hands-on time is minimal, but make them on a day when you can peek in the oven now and then.

Fried Rice

SERVES 5-6

INGREDIENTS

1 carrot
1 green or red pepper
1 whole white onion
1 celery stalk
4 Tablespoons oil
4 cloves garlic, minced
2 eggs, lightly beaten
2 cups cooked rice
2 Tablespoons soy sauce
2 Tablespoons sesame seeds (optional)

EQUIPMENT

measuring spoons (1 Tablespoon)
chef's knife
garlic press
saute pan

Saute the carrot, pepper, onion and celery in 2 Tablespoons oil until the onion is golden brown.

Add the garlic and saute for about a minute longer.

Push vegetables to the side of the pan and add the other 2 Tablespoons oil.

Pour the beaten eggs into the oil and stir until lightly scrambled.

Combine with the vegetables.

Add rice and mix well.

Dress rice with soy sauce and sesame seeds and serve.

You will recognize this as part of Dinner #2, often requested by Maisie.

Rosemary Roast Potatoes

SERVES 5-7

INGREDIENTS

5-7 yukon gold or russet Potatoes

½ cup olive oil

1 teaspoon salt

1 teaspoon pepper

2-3 sprigs fresh rosemary, stems stripped, leaves chopped

EQUIPMENT

baking pan

chef's knife and cutting board

measuring spoon (1 teaspoon)

large bowl for tossing potatoes with oil

spatula

Preheat oven to 400°F.

Slice potatoes lengthwise into ½" *fries* with skin still attached.

Toss them in a medium bowl with olive oil, salt, pepper and rosemary until all the pieces are evenly coated with oil.

Spread potato pieces on baking pan so that they are all in a single layer with no overlapping.

Bake until golden brown on the bottom, about 20 minutes.

Flip with spatula and continue to bake, golden side up, for another 15 minutes.

Adjust seasoning with salt and pepper, or other spices like onion powder, garlic powder or taco seasoning powder.

Remove from pan and place potatoes on paper towels to drain or serve directly from pan.

Another one of Dad's specialties.

Sauteed Broccoli

SERVES 5-6

INGREDIENTS

2 Tablespoons oil

1 broccoli crown, cut into florets and washed well

2 cloves garlic, minced

2 Tablespoons soy sauce

EQUIPMENT

measuring spoons (1 Tablespoon)

saute pan

chef's knife and cutting board

Heat 2 Tablespoons oil in a saute pan over high heat until a drop of water sizzles in the pan. (Nana would have spit in the pan: sizzling = sterilizing.)

Add the broccoli and saute for about a minute.

Add the garlic and stir constantly until the broccoli is bright green.

Splash the broccoli with soy sauce and serve hot.

If you were lucky, this recipe also was part of Dinner #2.

HOLIDAY

Hazelnut Raspberry Bouche de Noel

SERVES 6-8

INGREDIENTS

¾ cup flour
1 teaspoon baking powder
¼ teaspoon salt
5 eggs
¾ cup sugar
½ teaspoon vanilla
vegetable oil spray

EQUIPMENT

2 pieces parchment paper
10"x 15" baking pan
small bowl
flour sifter
mixer and medium bowl
rubber spatula
offset spatula
measuring cups
(¼ cup)
measuring spoons
(1 teaspoon, ½ teaspoon,
¼ teaspoon)

Preheat oven to 350°F.

Coat a baking pan with vegetable oil spray and cover with parchment. Spray the parchment lightly.

Sift the flour, baking powder and salt into a small bowl and set aside.

In a medium bowl, beat the eggs for 2 minutes until they are bubbly. Add the sugar and increase the speed. Beat 8 more minutes, adding vanilla at the last minute.

Using a rubber spatula, gently fold the flour mixture into the egg mixture until no flour streaks remain.

Pour the batter into the prepared pan, spreading it out to pan corners with an offset spatula and bake 15 minutes.

Invert the pan onto a second piece of parchment and peel off the pan lining. Quickly and gently, roll the short end of the cake – with the second sheet of parchment – until you have a fully rolled cake.

Let cool, seam side down, for 15 minutes.

Once cool, unroll gently and peel off parchment.

Spread filling evenly, (see recipe for Bouch de Noel – Filling and Frosting) all the way out to the edges, and re-roll tightly.

Chill.

I remember a lot of ribbing when Dad and I first tried to make this for Christmas. Up to that point, the menu starred the usual apple pie, pumpkin pie or maybe mince pie, but never a cake. Never a cake shaped like a log. We struggled with the 4 basic recipes (cake, filling, frosting and meringue mushrooms,) but "many hands make light work," as Baba used to say. Consider this a two person cake. It's both beautiful and delicious. Very French and very Christmassy.

Bouche de Noel Filling and Frosting

FROSTS AND FILLS ONE LOG

INGREDIENTS

2 sticks unsalted butter

1½ cups confectioner's sugar

¾ cup Nutella

1 Tablespoon half and half

½ cup raspberry jam

2 cups dark, unsweetened cocoa

1 teaspoon salt

EQUIPMENT

mixer

medium bowl

smaller bowl

measuring spoons (1 Tablespoon, 1 teaspoon)

measuring cups (1 cup, ¼ cup)

Combine first four ingredients and beat on medium speed for 2 minutes until smooth.

Remove half of base mixture to smaller bowl.

For filling, add jam to half of base mixture. Beat until smooth and chill.

For frosting, add cocoa and salt to other half of base mixture. Beat until smooth and chill.

Bring mixture to room temperature about an hour before filling or frosting.

To frost, cover filled cake roll evenly and drag a fork lengthwise down the cake for *bark* effect.

Reserve a small amount of frosting as "glue" to attach mushroom caps to the stems.

Garnish with Meringue Mushrooms (see recipe.)

Bouche de Noel Meringue Mushrooms

MAKES ABOUT 30

INGREDIENTS

¼ cup water

½ cup sugar

2 large egg whites

pinch salt

⅛ teaspoon cream of tartar

½ teaspoon vanilla extract

1 teaspoon cocoa

1 teaspoon confectioner's sugar

EQUIPMENT

parchment

2 rimmed baking sheets

candy thermometer

mixer or whisk and bowl

saucepan

pastry bag and ¼" tip

measuring spoons (½ teaspoon, ⅛ teaspoon)

measuring cups (½ cup, ¼ cup)

Preheat oven to 200°F.

Line 2 rimmed baking sheets with parchment paper.

Combine water and sugar in heavy saucepan. Cover and bring to boil over medium-high heat. Boil, swirling pan once or twice, until sugar has dissolved – 2 minutes. If necessary, wipe down any sugar crystals on side of pan with damp pastry brush. Cook, uncovered, until temperature registers 238°F on candy thermometer, about 10 minutes.

While sugar is cooking, beat egg whites until frothy, about 1 minute. Add salt and cream of tartar and beat, gradually increasing speed to high. until whites hold soft peaks, about 1 minute. With beaters at medium speed, slowly pour hot syrup into egg whites, avoiding whisk. Increase speed to medium-high and continue to beat until meringue comes to room temperature and becomes very thick and shiny, 5-10 minutes.

Using rubber spatula, fold in vanilla.

Fit pastry bag with ¼" pastry tip and fill with meringue. Pipe about 30 mushroom cap shapes and an equal number of mushroom stem shapes onto prepared pans.

Bake meringue for 2 hours. Turn off oven, and leave meringue in oven until very dry and crisp, about 30 minutes longer.

Cool mushroom caps and stems on baking sheets.

Using frosting, glue caps to stems and place around log with greens and berries as garnish. Dust mushrooms with cocoa powder. Dust entire log and garnishes with confectioner's sugar.

Cranberry Relish Vermont Style

SERVES 10-12

INGREDIENTS

1 bag fresh cranberries, washed

1 whole orange, washed, with skin on but stem and seeds removed, quartered

1 teaspoon Chinese Five Spice powder or cardamon (optional)

½ cup maple syrup

½ cup sugar

EQUIPMENT

measuring cups (½ cup)

measuring spoons (1 teaspoon)

food processor

serving dish

Toss the berries and the orange pieces in a food processor. Pulse until the fruit is in small, uniform chunks.

Add the spice, syrup and sugar and pulse again until fully mixed.

Add to serving bowl and refrigerate, covered, until serving.

This recipe is a little easier than cooked cranberry sauce but just as good. It doesn't require cooking, but there will be dishes to wash.

Mushroom and Green Bean Casserole

SERVES 10-12

INGREDIENTS

2 cups day-old breadcrumbs

2 Tablespoons unsalted butter, softened

¼ teaspoon salt

⅛ teaspoon pepper

3 cups fried onions, canned

1 Tablespoon salt

2 pounds green beans, trimmed and halved

3 Tablespoons unsalted butter

1 pound white mushrooms, stems removed, roughly chopped

3 cloves garlic, minced

¾ teaspoon salt

⅛ teaspoon pepper

3 tablespoons flour

1½ cups chicken broth

1½ cups heavy cream

EQUIPMENT

food processor or pastry blender

Dutch oven

13"x 9" baking dish

bowl for ice and paper towels

measuring cups (1 cup, ½ cup)

measuring spoons (1 Tablespoon, 1 teaspoon, ¼ teaspoon, ⅛ teaspoon)

colander

Using a fork, combine bread, butter, salt, and pepper until mixture resembles coarse crumbs.

Toss with onions and set aside.

Preheat oven to 425°F.

Fill large bowl with cold water.

Bring 4 quarts water to boil in large Dutch oven.

Add 1 Tablespoon salt and beans. Cook beans until bright green and crisp-tender, about 6 minutes.

Drain beans in colander and plunge immediately into cold water to stop cooking.

Spread beans on paper towels.

Add butter to now empty Dutch oven and melt over medium-high heat. Add mushrooms, garlic, ¾ teaspoon salt, and ⅛ teaspoon pepper; cook until mushrooms release moisture and liquid evaporates, about 12 minutes.

Add flour and cook for 1 minute, stirring constantly.

Stir in broth and bring to simmer, stirring constantly.

Add cream, reduce heat to medium, and simmer until sauce is thickened and reduced, about 12 minutes.

Season with salt and pepper to taste.

Add green beans to sauce and stir until evenly coated.

Arrange in even layer in baking dish.

Sprinkle with bread crumb topping and bake until top is golden brown and sauce is bubbling around edges, about 15 minutes.

Serve immediately.

Both Thanksgiving and Christmas menus need some green vegetables. Traditionally, this recipe called for cream of mushroom soup and canned green beans. Here it uses fresh ingredients.

Roast Beef with Crispy Potatoes

SERVES 10-12

INGREDIENTS

4 pound beef tenderloin, tied well

1 cup bread crumbs

1 teaspoon salt

1 teaspoon pepper

4 Tablespoons plus 2 teaspoons vegetable oil

2 shallots, minced

4 Tablespoons horseradish, strained of liquid

2 Tablespoons minced parsley

1 potato, baked, cooked, peeled and sliced

1½ teaspoons mayonnaise

1½ teaspoons Dijon mustard

½ teaspoon gelatin

EQUIPMENT

saute pan

roasting pan and rack

chef's knife and cutting board

strainer

rimmed baking sheet

measuring spoons (1 Tablespoon, 1 teaspoon, ½ teaspoon)

measuring cups (1 cup)

Sprinkle beef with ½ teaspoon salt, cover with plastic wrap, and let stand for 30 minutes.

Toast bread crumbs with 2 teaspoons oil, ½ teaspoon salt, and ½ teaspoon pepper on a rimmed baking sheet for 5 minutes.

Once cool, toss bread crumbs with shallots, 2 Tablespoons horseradish and parsley.

Saute potato slices in 2 Tablespoons oil until golden brown, then drain on paper towel.

Once dry, chop until coarsely ground. Toss with breadcrumb mixture and spread in roasting pan.

Unwrap beef and pat dry. Sprinkle evenly with remaining ½ teaspoon pepper.

Heat 2 Tablespoons oil in saute pan over medium-high heat until just smoking.

Sear tenderloin until well browned on all sides, 5-7 minutes.

Transfer to wire rack set in roasting pan and let cool.

Combine remaining 2 Tablespoons horseradish, mayonnaise, and mustard in small bowl. Just before you're ready to coat the beef, add gelatin and stir to combine.

Spread paste on top of beef. Roll in bread-crumb mixture, pressing gently so crumbs adhere.

Return beef to wire rack. Roast 30 minutes then rest 20 minutes.

Carefully cut meat into ½" thick slices and serve.

The centerpiece of many Christmas dinners, before we started going out for Chinese.

Cranberry Cornbread Stuffing

SERVES 8-10

INGREDIENTS

1½ cups gluten-free flour

1½ cups cornmeal

⅓ cup sugar

2 teaspoons baking powder

1 teaspoon baking soda

1 teaspoon salt

2 eggs

2 Tablespoons maple syrup

1½ cups whole milk or cream

6 Tablespoons unsalted butter, melted and cooled

1 pound McKenzie bulk sausage

3 shallots, chopped coarsely

1 cup celery, chopped coarsely

1 Tablespooon Herbes de Provence or Bell's Turkey seasoning

1-2 cups chicken broth

2 cups dried cranberries

EQUIPMENT

measuring cups
(1 cup, ½ cup, ⅓ cup)

measuring spoons
(1 Tablespoon, 1 teaspoon)

8" square baking pan

whisk

toothpick

chef's knife and cutting board

saute pan

Dutch oven

foil

bowl for dry ingredients

bowl for wet ingredients

9"x 13" baking pan

spatula

Preheat the oven to 350°F.

Butter a 8"x 8" baking pan.

For the cornbread, whisk together dry ingredients in a large bowl and set aside. In a separate bowl, whisk eggs with other wet ingredients.

Pour wet ingredients into dry ingredients and stir just enough to combine.

Bake 25-30 minutes or until toothpick comes out clean. Cool.

Invert cornbread onto cutting board and cut into 1" pieces. Toast the pieces in a 9"x 13" baking pan for 30 minutes, flipping the pieces once to brown both sides.

Saute McKenzie's sausage, breaking it into bite sized pieces, for about 15 minutes.

Remove sausage from pan and add shallots, celery and seasoning and sauté until cooked but still crunchy.

Stir sausage mixture into cornbread pan and stir well. Add cranberries and stir to distribute.

Heat broth in Dutch oven and add sausage and cornbread mixture. Toss to combine.

Cover and bake at 325°F for 30 minutes just before serving.

A tradition which we modified when Maisie went gluten-free.

Lobster Bisque

SERVES 6

INGREDIENTS

3 pounds lobster meat, cooked, shelled and chopped

6 Tablespoons unsalted butter

1 carrot, chopped fine

1 stalk celery, chopped fine

1 white onion, chopped fine

1 clove garlic, minced

½ cup flour

4 8 ounce bottles clam juice

1 14½ ounce can diced tomatoes, drained

1 cup heavy cream

1 Tablespoon lemon juice

pinch cayenne

1 Tablespoon dry sherry (optional)

salt and ground black pepper

EQUIPMENT

measuring cups (1 cup, ½ cup)

measuring spoons (1 Tablespoon)

chef's knife and cutting board

Dutch oven

whisk

Heat 2 Tablespoons butter in a large Dutch oven over medium heat until foaming.

Add the carrot, celery, onion, and garlic and cook, stirring frequently, until the vegetables are slightly softened and lightly browned, 6-7 minutes.

Add the remaining 4 Tablespoons of butter and stir until melted.

Whisk in the flour, stirring constantly, until combined thoroughly, about 1 minute.

Slowly stir in clam juice and tomatoes and bring liquid to a boil.

Cover the pot, reduce the heat to low, and simmer, stirring until thickened, about 20 minutes.

Stir in the cream and simmer for 10 minutes longer.

Stir in the lemon juice and cayenne.

Bring to a simmer over medium-high heat. When piping hot, add the diced lobster meat and sherry and then season to taste with salt and pepper.

Serve immediately.

We really shouldn't have added this to the Christmas dinner menu at the last minute but I'm glad we did because the recipe is superb.

Stuffed Mushrooms

SERVES 12

INGREDIENTS

2 pounds large white mushrooms (about 20)

1 box chicken-flavored Stovetop Stuffing

¼ cup onion, minced

¼ cup red pepper, minced

¼ cup sausage, cooked and crumbled (optional)

EQUIPMENT

measuring cups (¼ cup)

medium spoon

chef's knife and cutting board

mixing bowl

large baking pan

Preheat the oven to 350°F.

Wash mushrooms well. Snap off stems.

Using a Tablespoon, scoop out just enough of the underside of the mushroom cap to hold some stuffing.

Make the stuffing according to package directions.

Mix in onion, red pepper and sausage.

Let stand.

Fill mushroom caps with stuffing mixture.

Set filled mushrooms on large baking pan, stuffing side up.

Bake 20 minutes.

Filling may rise up out of mushrooms, but it will settle back down again as they cool.

Use a sharp spatula to release mushrooms from pan so they don't tear.

Think back to Christmas 2009. Grandpa and Elvie came up from Florida Nana and Baba came over from Morristown to Morris Township. I added this hors d'oeuvre to our usual Christmas menu for a change of pace and it became tradition.

	Gluten Free	Paleo	Vegetarian
Almond Thumbprint Cookies			■
Apple Pie			■
Applejack Bars			■
Baked Apples	■	■	■
Baguettes			■
Banana Bread			■
Basic Dijon Vinaigrette	■	■	■
Blueberry Muffins			■
Bouche de Noel: Filling and Frosting	■		■
Brisket	■	■	
Butterscotch Candy	■		■
Carrot Cake			■
Chicken Chili	■	■	
Chicken and Rice	■	■	
Chocolate Raspberry Cheesecake Brownies			■
Chocolate Sugar-Dusted Cookies			■
Chocolate Stout Cake			■
Classic Mac & Cheese with Vermont Cheddar			■
Cole Slaw	■	■	■
Cranberry Cornbread Stuffing	■		
Cranberry Relish Vermont Style	■	■	■
Dad's Tortilla Soup	■	■	
Dewars Apple Cake			■
Fig Cookies			■
Flank Steak Satay	■	■	
Fried Rice	■	■	■
Hazlenut Raspberry Bouche de Noel			■
Jalapeno Red Onion Relish	■	■	■
Lemon Layer Cake			■
Leslie Mandel's Jewish Chicken Soup	■	■	
Mahogany Baked Beans	■	■	
Meringue Mushrooms for Buche de Noel	■		■
Mexican Chicken Soup		■	
Mojo Pork	■	■	
Mrs. Massengill's Salad Dressing	■	■	
Paella	■	■	
Peanut Butter & Jelly Swirl Blondies	■		■
Pecan Coffee Cake			■
Portable Chicken	■	■	
Popcorn Balls from Cranny	■		■
Rosemary Roast Potatoes	■	■	■
Roast Beef with Crispy Potatoes	■	■	
SS France Croissants			■
Salad Nicoise	■	■	
Sauteed Broccoli	■	■	■
St. George's Day Cookie Bars			■
Strawberry Marmalade	■		■
Terry Delano's Hot Fudge Sauce	■		■

Kate Laud lives in Shelburne, Vermont with her Bernese Mountain Dog, Winnie, Nell, the cat, and various grown millennial children. She spent her career in banking and finance, but has always enjoyed food, entertaining and experimenting in the kitchen.

Kate is married to cartoonist and private equity consultant, Paul Laud, who lives in Connecticut and provides the humorous banter that has been a backdrop to their lives. Their children, Matt, Charlie and Maisie, amp up the laughter and, like most families, when they are together, it usually involves food.

www.ingramcontent.com/pod-product-compliance
Lightning Source LLC
Chambersburg PA
CBHW061403160426
42811CB00100D/1435